Java Cryptography Extensions

The Morgan Kaufmann Practical Guides Series

Series Editor: Michael J. Donahoo

Java Cryptography Extensions: Practical Guide for Programmers
Jason Weiss

JSP: Practical Guide for Java Programmers
Robert J. Brunner

JSTL: Practical Guide for JSP Programmers
Sue Spielman

Java: Practical Guide for Programmers
Zbigniew M. Sikora

The Struts Framework: Practical Guide for Java Programmers
Sue Spielman

Multicast Sockets: Practical Guide for Programmers
David Makofske and Kevin Almeroth

TCP/IP Sockets in Java: Practical Guide for Programmers
Kenneth L. Calvert and Michael J. Donahoo

TCP/IP Sockets in C: Practical Guide for Programmers
Michael J. Donahoo and Kenneth L. Calvert

JDBC: Practical Guide for Java Programmers
Gregory D. Speegle

For further information on these books and for a list of forthcoming titles,
please visit our website at http://www.mkp.com/practical

Java Cryptography Extensions

Practical Guide for Programmers

Jason Weiss

AMSTERDAM · BOSTON · HEIDELBERG · LONDON
NEW YORK · OXFORD · PARIS · SAN DIEGO
SAN FRANCISCO · SINGAPORE · SYDNEY · TOKYO

Morgan Kaufmann is an imprint of Elsevier

ELSEVIER

MORGAN KAUFMANN PUBLISHERS

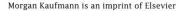

Senior Editor	Rick Adams
Publishing Services Manager	Andre Cuello
Project Manager	Anne B. McGee
Associate Editor	Karyn Johnson
Cover Design	Yvo Reizebos Design
Cover Image	Image #939879: © BananaStock/BananaStock, Ltd./ PictureQuest
Composition	CEPHA Imaging Pvt. Ltd.
Technical Illustration	Dartmouth Publishing, Inc.
Copyeditor	Graphic World Publishing Services
Proofreader	Graphic World Publishing Services
Indexer	Graphic World Publishing Services
Interior printer	The Maple-Vail Book Manufacturing Group
Cover printer	Phoenix Color Corp.

Morgan Kaufmann Publishers is an imprint of Elsevier.
500 Sansome Street, Suite 400, San Francisco, CA 94111

This book is printed on acid-free paper.

Library of Congress Cataloging-in-Publication Data

Weiss, Jason.
 Java cryptography extensions : practical guide for programmers / Jason Weiss.
   p. cm.
 Includes bibliographical references and index.
 ISBN 0-12-742751-1
  1. Java (Computer program language) 2. Cryptography. I. Title.

 QA76.73.J38W445 2004
 005.8'2--dc22

                                                                2003070900

For information on all Morgan Kaufmann publications,
visit our Web site at *www.mkp.com*.

Printed in the United States of America
04 05 06 07 08   5 4 3 2 1

For my wife Meredith and our son Kyle,

whom I love more dearly than anything else

Contents

Preface

I've always exhibited a deep enthusiasm for computers and software development. In fact, I wrote some of my first software applications before I finished the sixth grade. However, it wasn't until I joined the U.S. Navy as a Cryptologic Technician that I became interested in cryptography, or more specifically cryptanalysis. Most people oversimplify cryptography. "Yeah, we're secure; we encrypt our data."

That Means Nothing.

How strong is the key? What is the key's effective bit size? Which cipher mode was employed? How are you managing the key(s)? Did you use the right type of cipher for the job at hand? Is the data padded? Are you merely storing the data in an encrypted state, or are you broadcasting it across a network?

People also often are confused about where the boundaries of cryptography lie. Generally, the field of cryptography includes encryption, one-way hashes, digital signatures, and various digital-certificate–related technologies (becaue the certificates are built around keys typically used in either digital signature or encryption operations). Authentication is only associated with cryptography, for example, to the extent of the inherent relationship that exists between a public and private key pair and that if the public key can decipher that signature, then we've authenticated that the private key had to be used in the encryption of that hash. Authorization is certainly well beyond the boundaries of cryptography, so don't expect any discussion of Access Control Lists (ACL) or group management here. If you are looking for this type of material, you should look into the Java Authentication and Authorization Specification (JAAS).

One of the early challenges I faced when I started designing and writing software that employed cryptographic algorithms was making sense of it all. There seemed to be an endless stream of terminology! What is the difference between Electronic Codebook Mode and Cipher Block Chaining? How do I know if I should choose a symmetric cipher over an asymmetric cipher? And once I understood the differences between these and knew to choose a symmetric cipher, I was still faced with the daunting task of picking *which* symmetric cipher to use, that is, which physical implementation of a symmetric cipher.

Identifying that you need some form of cryptography in your application is elementary. Even an executive-type can make a statement like "boy, we better protect that data!" Where to go from there is the major challenge.

Target Audience

This book is intended for software engineers who are experienced in Java but have little to no experience with cryptography. I assume that if you're holding this book you have an advanced understanding of terms like *authentication, digital certificate, public key, encryption*, and so on. We will review more advanced topics, such as cipher modes, padding structures, and so on, where applicable.

Cryptography is an "on-demand" programming exercise for most engineers. On demand, it is coded once and tested, and then focus shifts to the business problem for the next *n* months of the project. As a result, it's very easy for even the most experienced Java engineer to become rusty on cryptographic concepts, because they aren't used on a daily basis. This book will address this problem head on, keeping definitions and code examples at your fingertips for times when they are needed.

This book was planned and written to solve two distinct problems that software engineers face after they reach the conclusion that they need to employ some form of a cryptographic architecture in their design. First, cryptography is a world unto itself, in which most texts present complex mathematical calculations *ad nauseum*. As professional software engineers, we face increasingly tighter deadlines and simply don't have the time to fully understand the underlying mathematical theorems at work behind an algorithm. While the underlying math is *very* important, we'll leave that work to the researchers at universities around the world. I openly admit that there are many researchers who possess mathematical skills exponentially greater than mine, and *they* can explain to you why the algorithm I'm using—which passed public scrutiny at *their* level—is considered cryptographically secure. Thus, I've worked very hard to gloss over mathematical concepts, and included references where applicable to sources that can provide insight into the mathematics if you're so inclined. However, we still have a responsibility to become fluent in the terminology of the cryptographic universe if we are going to make informed design decisions. This text will help you achieve the minimum fluency requirement for the language of cryptography by discussing the various cryptographic engines that are exposed via the Java Cryptology Architecture (JCA) and the Java Cryptography Extensions (JCE).

Once you employ your cryptographic fluency and determine that your design requires a block cipher using a 128-bit key PKCS#5 padding and a CBC cipher mode, you suddenly realize that scope and magnitude of your second problem; how do I write *that* in Java *quickly*? This is the second distinct problem this book intends to help you solve.

To accomplish this, a substantial amount of time was spent to provide real-world code samples in discrete pieces that you can choose from *a la carte.* Ideally you'll just copy and paste the code I've written into your code and expand it/customize it from there.

Code Examples

Sun's JDK 1.4.1 release was used to author all of the code examples you hold here. The development was done primarily on an Apple PowerMac G4, and testing was done on a Windows XP box as well. Approximately 75% of these samples work with an unextended version of the JCA/JCE, but other more complex algorithms like RSA encryption require the download and installation of a 3rd-party JCE provider. To download the code examples in .zip format, access http://www.mkp.com and find this book's page by searching in the online catalogue.

There is a close relationship between the code example's JavaDocs and the book. Each code sample explicitly points back to the section in the book, making it easy to locate the corresponding text that explains the sample. For clarity, code examples in the early chapters have been entirely self-contained, including coding techniques not directly related to the material being discussed, like Java I/O operations. Later in the book a single utility class is incorporated into the code examples. The reason for this utility class is twofold: to shrink the size of the code examples and to allow you to focus on the material at hand (not Java I/O). The following is a partial listing of the helper methods present in this class, and the names give an indication of their relationship to Java I/O operations:

- loadPublicKey()
- readCipherTextFile()
- readFromSocketChannel()
- readPlainTextFile()
- byte2Hex()
- toByteArray()
- toHexString()
- writeCipherTextFile()

You may choose to include this utility class in your application, or copy/paste pertinent methods from it into an existing utility class your application may already define.

Each code sample expands each exception that might be thrown into its own code block. This was done intentionally, for two reasons. First, when you paste the code you won't have to hunt around the JavaDocs to locate all of the exceptions you need to catch for the code you're using. And perhaps more importantly, to encourage you to take that extra three minutes to use Java's robust exception-handling architecture properly instead of just catching everything using a lonely catch (Exception e) code block.

To make it easier for you to reuse the code samples in your application, when applicable, code examples either declare or have commented out dynamic registration of both the Legion of the Bouncy Castle JCE Provider and the Cryptix JCE Provider. This provides both the code fragment to register the provider so you don't have to look it up, and more importantly, a visual cue that the algorithm you need to use is probably not natively supported by Sun's JDK 1.4.1 and will require an extra .jar file when you deploy.

Whenever a 3rd-party JCE provider was required, the code arbitrarily chose to dynamically register the providers in positions 5 and 6, respectively. The code samples can be built using Apache Ant. For documentation on how to use Apache Ant, see http://ant.apache.org. Whenever the samples need to perform file access, they refer to the root directory. Depending upon your permissions (especially if you are using a *nix system) you may need to adjust these paths to be rooted in your home directory.

Throughout the text I refer to the Java SDK as $JAVA_HOME. Since this is a developer-oriented book, it is assumed that you have the complete SDK installed and not simply a Java Runtime Environment (JRE). When moving to a production environment where the SDK may not be available, be sure to substitute $JAVA_HOME/jre/lib/ext with $JRE_HOME/lib/ext where applicable. For consistency, throughout the text we use $JAVA_HOME notation.

Code examples use a smaller 9 point Courier font like this throughout the text. In the longer code examples (specifically the KeyAgreement examples) key blocks have been identified with a 15% gray shade and individual labels. The labels are referred to specifically in the body of the text.

Acknowledgments

It is impossible for an individual to author a book like this without some help. In particular I would like to thank my acquiring editor Karyn Johnson and my technical editor Jeff Donahoo for their invaluable feedback and guidance throughout the entire process. Special thanks go out to Reed Shilts for reviewing and verifying the code samples provided with the book for completeness, accuracy, and cross-platform "gotchas" that I failed to catch when I initially wrote them. I'd also like to thank all of the following reviewers who provided great feedback on the draft chapters: Michael Parks, Uwe Guenther, Anthony Nadalin, and Jon Eaves. Their input helped to shape the book you hold in your hands today.

Organization of this Book

Chapter 1 focuses on introducing the Java Cryptography Architecture and the Java Cryptography Extensions. Additionally, it demonstrates the usefulness of the Security and Provider classes.

Chapter 2 centers on symmetric cryptography operations, including the generation of cryptographically secure pseudo-random number generators (CSPRNG), generation of secret keys, and working with the Cipher engine.

Chapter 3 builds on our knowledge of how the Cipher engine works, introducing asymmetric ciphers. A discussion of key agreements between 2 or more parties is also included in this chapter.

Chapter 4 introduces the message digests, message authentication codes and digital signatures. The theme of this chapter is how to ensure the content of a document didn't change.

Chapter 5 details the uses of a key store for tracking secret keys, key pairs and digital certificates. It also demonstrates how digital certificates can be used for encryption.

Finally

For those of you who like really hard puzzles, here are cryptographic puzzles that pay you cash prizes for winning:

http://www.rsasecurity.com/rsalabs/challenges

These contests directly attest to the differences in strengths between symmetric and asymmetric algorithms and the inability to effectively compare one to the other. If this book exposes an excitement about cryptology you never knew was in you, I encourage you to nurture your curiosity. For learning the history of codes and ciphers, one of the best books I've found on this topic is by Fred B. Wrixon, titled *Codes and Ciphers & Other Cryptic & Clandestine Communication*, published by Black Dog & Leventhal Publishers, ISBN 1-57912-040-7.

## chapter 1

Understanding Java's Cryptographic Architecture

Cryptography has its roots in very complex (and often theoretical) mathematics. As a result, computers and cryptography complement each other well. Today's advanced cryptographic operations involve mind-boggling amounts of mathematical calculations, and computers perform these calculations exponentially faster than a human can perform them by hand. The Java language includes a well-defined architecture that allows you to include cryptographic services in your designs without fully comprehending the mathematical proofs or calculations behind the algorithms. However, this does not mean that it is not important to understand the algorithms (i.e., the cryptographic tools) at your disposal. As an analogy, a screwdriver is a wonderful tool for driving a wood screw into a piece of wood; however, that same screwdriver would not be effective if the object being driven was a finishing nail.

Performing cryptographic operations with Java does not involve hundreds of lines of code or require a Ph.D. in mathematics from MIT. Perhaps the most visible aspect of cryptography is encryption, which can be accomplished in Java using as little as seven lines of code, not counting proper exception handling. Here is a brief example demonstrating a simple encryption operation. Don't worry about comprehending every aspect of the program just yet—we have the whole book to explore Java's cryptographic capabilities!

NOTE: Please review the preface for code style information and download instructions.

Example 1.1 Sample Code Location: com.mkp.jce.chap1.SmallExample

---

```
try
{
```

1

```java
//Lookup a key generator for the DES cipher
KeyGenerator kg = KeyGenerator.getInstance("DES");

//Generate a secret key that can be used by the DES cipher
SecretKey key = kg.generateKey();
SecretKeySpec keySpec = new SecretKeySpec(key.getEncoded(), "DES");

//Lookup an instance of a DES cipher
Cipher cipher = Cipher.getInstance("DES");

//Initialize the cipher using the secret key
cipher.init(Cipher.ENCRYPT_MODE, keySpec);

//Encrypt our message
String plainText = "This is a secret message";
byte[] cipherText = cipher.doFinal(plainText.getBytes());

System.out.println("Resulting Cipher Text:n");
for(int i=0;i<cipherText.length;i++)
{
        System.out.print(cipherText[i] + " ");
}
System.out.println("");

} catch (Exception e)
{
    e.printStackTrace();
}
```

This example demonstrates some of the core tenets of cryptography with Java in action. It shows the creation of a secret key that is used to translate an unencrypted message into

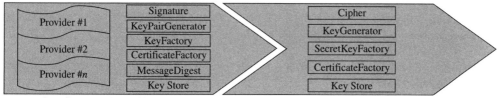

Figure 1.1: Java's cryptographic libraries.

an encrypted one. The output of this sample will differ each time it is run because the key is essentially random; when I ran it the output looked like this:

```
Resulting Cipher Text:
106 93 20 33 -86 -110 109 87  57 31 95 5 -67 36 -39 -7 117 -50 119 -26 -51 -40
118 105 68 5 -29 -47 -90 -89 -70 84
```

The example also demonstrates the use of *engine classes*, classes that are not instantiated directly. Alas, we do not want to get ahead of ourselves, so we will rewind and start by defining Java's cryptographic infrastructure.

1.1 Java and Cryptography

From its humble birth through its present day incarnation, the Java language continues to offer developers a computing platform that swells with cryptographic functionality. Because of U.S. export laws at the time, the functionality is split between two different libraries, the JAVA Cryptography Architecture (JCA) and the Java Cryptography Extensions (JCE). Figure 1.1 shows the relationship between these two cryptographic libraries, displaying some of the capabilities covered throughout this book. The first library, JCA, is tightly integrated with the core Java APIs. The second library, JCE, builds off of the concepts and capabilities found in the JCA. The JCE houses many of the advanced cryptographic operations that were previously under U.S. export control. However, the political landscape has changed, and as of JDK 1.4, the JCA and JCE are present "out of the box" without requiring a separate download of the JCE. JCE 1.2.2 remains available as a separate download for JDK 1.2 and 1.3 installations, and it supports the same suite of engines found in JDK 1.4.

Cryptography is often associated with the sole process of encryption/decryption; however, the true scope of the field is actually much larger than this, encompassing a wide array of operations to include:

- Message digests or hashing
- Message authentication codes
- Digital signatures

- Digital certificates

- Cryptographically secure random numbers

- Secret key generation and storage

- Key agreements

- Encryption/decryption

Clearly the field of cryptology spans much more than just encryption/decryption. One notable absence is Base64 encoding, which is not encryption and not considered part of the field of cryptography. The act of applying a Base64 encoding to a document does not suffice as a form of hiding sensitive data. Base64 encoding is documented in an RFC [4], and was designed to convert 8-bit binary data into a 6-bit printable representation. For more details on Base64 encoding, see Appendix A.

Before we can adequately discuss calling cryptography operations from within a Java class, it is imperative developers have a firm grasp on the infrastructure Java provides to make these operations possible. The JCA serves as the proverbial cornerstone of Java's cryptographic architecture, and it is the most logical place to start.

1.2 Java Cryptography Architecture

Security, in particular cryptography, has always been a core API of Java, located in and below the java.security package. The JCA was explicitly designed to provide and expose cryptographic operations to developers in need of such functionality. The advent of the Java2 SDK revealed a substantially improved JCA architecture, and we won't spend too much time living in the past discussing the way it used to be before the facelift. The architects of the JCA were given several broad but guiding design principles that had to be met.

- Algorithm independence

- Algorithm extensibility

- Implementation independence

- Implementation interoperability

Developers who require the use of cryptographic operations in their code dramatically benefit from these design principles. In fact, the elegance of the final design lies in its ability to let the developer decide what level of interaction they want to have with the underlying mechanics of the JCA, that is, a little or a lot. For example, developers can simply request a message digest, or they can be extremely specific and indicate that they require a *specific* message digest from an explicitly named **cryptographic service provider**, or simply a *provider*. A provider implements one or more Java packages that declare concrete implementations of well-known cryptographic features, like a key store that serves as the physical repository for secret keys and key pairs. While there will be the presence of Java classes included with the provider implementation, it is possible that their complete solution encompasses software and hardware. For example, the provider may use a Smart Card as the physical key store repository, and their key store implementation (software) knows how to interact with the Smart Card reader (hardware) attached to the computer.

The first guiding characteristic of the JCA architecture was **Algorithm independence**, which serves as a mechanism to classify cryptographic operations into well-known (read well-documented) categories. The JCA refers to each category as an *engine*, which is simply another name for a Java class. To ensure consistency between this book and the JCA documentation, we will use the engine nomenclature. The following is a complete list of engines found in the JCA:

- **MessageDigest** produces a hash value for a given message
- **Signature** produces a digital signature of a document
- **KeyPairGenerator** produces a pair of keys that, for example, could sign a document
- **KeyFactory** breaks down a key into its discrete parts and vice versa
- **KeyStore** manages and stores various secret keys and key pairs
- **SecureRandom** produces random numbers suitable for use in cryptology
- **AlgorithmParameters** manages the encoding and decoding of the parameters for a given cryptographic algorithm
- **AlgorithmParameterGenerator** generates a complete set of parameters required for a given cryptographic algorithm
- **CertificateFactory** creates public key certificates and certificate revocation lists
- **CertPathBuilder** establishes relationship chains between certificates
- **CertStore** manages and stores certificates and certificate revocation lists

Each of these engines will be discussed in more detail and used throughout the text. To provide a high level of algorithm independence, each JCA engine uses the **factory design pattern**, as documented by Gamma et al in their landmark work [19]. Essentially, each engine uses a factory method design, where the method is always declared static. Each factory method always returns back to the engine class itself (section 1.4 will briefly explore the *Service Provider Interface* [SPI] that provider's follow to see how this mechanism actually works). Here are two small code examples that demonstrate accessing the MessageDigest engine to obtain instances of different message digest algorithms (the algorithm parameter passed into any JCA or JCE engine is always case-insensitive):

```
MessageDigest md5Implementation = MessageDigest.getInstance("MD5");

MessageDigest sha1Implementation = MessageDigest.getInstance("SHA-1");
```

The decision by the JCA architects to use this design pattern in each engine class benefits developers and providers. As you read this, ongoing research on cryptographic operations is occurring at universities and cutting-edge companies around the globe. Providers can rest assured this research translates into newer, more powerful algorithms that can easily be accessed by Java developers around the globe. Developers benefit from the design because they do not have to worry about being locked into either single provider or obsolete algorithms. This leads into JCA's next design goal.

A by-product of the JCA's algorithm independence is its ability to support **algorithm extensibility**, which, simply stated, provides a mechanism for adding new algorithms that can be classified and exposed through one of the supported engines. Why should you be forced to use one and only one implementation of a cryptographic function? You should not. Algorithm extensibility can be thought of as capitalism for cryptographic algorithm engineers. If someone can successfully write a message digest that is five times faster and more collision-resistant to a greater bit-length than existing message digest implementations, then it should be extremely easy to access this new algorithm. Let's revisit the MessageDigest engine and see how we would access a new state-of-the-art message digest:

```
MessageDigest fastImplementation = MessageDigest.getInstance("SuperFastHash");
```

Implementation independence represents the notion that developers should be free to simply say "I need an MD5 message digest" and immediately get an instance of a class that provides such functionality without requiring the invocation of a slue of provider specific methods. Implementation independence essentially offers the developer a choice of how to handle the presence of providers. Each of the earlier MessageDigest engine examples was implementation independent, but in some rare cases the developer may choose to waive this property and explicitly request a named provider. This example requests that the BC provider's MD5 message digest implementation be returned:

```
MessageDigest bcMd5Implementation = MessageDigest.getInstance("MD5", "BC");
```

The Sun Java Runtime Environment (JRE) includes the SUN provider that implements one or more solutions for each of the JCA engines. However, it can't be stressed enough that the very nature of the JCA's architecture gives developers the opportunity to plug-in additional providers. Each provider determines what physical cryptographic implementations they wish to include in their solution. Theoretically, a provider may decide to only provide a single logical implementation of a random number generator, or they may opt to include a full spectrum of solutions for every engine.

> NOTE: Throughout the rest of the text the term "developer" will refer to the downstream software engineer, that is, you or I. The term "provider" will refer to the upstream software engineer, that is, the engineers who developed the SUN provider that comes with the JCA.

There are numerous third party providers on the market; some are open source and others are commercial frameworks that require licensing. In the open source community, two popular choices include implementations from The Legion of the Bouncy Castle (http://www.bouncycastle.org) and Cryptix (http://www.cryptix.org). I will stop short of recommending a specific provider here, and the book's code examples will use a mixture of implementations from open source providers. Sun's web site also publishes a list of providers at http://java.sun.com/products/jce/jce122_providers.html.

Along the same vein as implementation independence is implementation interoperability. **Implementation interoperability** is probably best defined through an example. Let's say there is a document that must be digitally signed. The developer might use provider A to generate a key pair, passing that key pair along to provider B's signature algorithm. Despite the fact that two different providers are being used, the pieces and parts that represent the whole cryptographic operation are interchangeable without any special action required by the developer.

Through careful planning, the JCA architects created a very robust foundation from which more advanced cryptographic operations could be exposed. Next we'll take a look at JCE and how they build on the JCA design.

1.3 Java Cryptography Extension (JCE)

Strictly speaking, the JCE extends the JCA by simply exposing more engines and including an additional provider, the SUNJCE provider, that includes one or more implementations for each engine. Recall that the separation between the JCA and the JCE was a result of political situations, not technical limitations. The JCE places its classes in a different package, javax.crypto.*, and it has several idiosyncrasies as we'll see shortly. We've already seen what engines the JCA includes, now let's shift our focus to the JCE engines. The following engines are specific to the JCE:

- **Cipher** performs encryption and decryption operations

- **KeyGenerator** produces secret keys used by ciphers

- **SecretKeyFactory** similar to the JCA's KeyFactory, but operate exclusively on SecretKey instances

- **KeyAgreement** embodies a key agreement protocol for multiple parties to dynamically create a shared secret among them

- **Mac** provides message authentication code functionality

Together, the JCA and the JCE represent a complete cryptographic platform. However, this platform is not without its idiosyncrasies. A common criticism often cited is that the disjunction between the JCA and the JCE is too visible. Developers are forced to remember which package an engine resides in—is it a JCA engine located in the java.security package or is it a JCE engine located in javax.crypto package? Another less obvious architectural difference lies in the class hierarchy. The JCA follows a stringent pattern, where the abstract engine class, e.g., Engine, extends another class with an identical name and SPI suffix, e.g., EngineSpi. The JCE, however, doesn't follow this pattern. For example, the

JCE Cipher engine neither declares itself abstract nor does it extend the CipherSpi class. Despite these differences, fortunately the key concept—looking up an engine implementation via a factory method—remains in tack. Recently, there have been calls to refactor these libraries into a single, more consistent library, especially since the political boundaries that existed have been removed and both libraries ship as part of JDK 1.4.

Overlooking these differences between the JCA and JCE, it is important to have at least a rudimentary understanding of the underlying architecture a provider must implement. Providers follow a strict set of rules defined by the SPI. The next section will provide developers with a high level understanding of the SPI.

1.4 Understanding the Service Provider Interface Architecture

Our goal in this section is *not* to discuss the Service Provider Interface (SPI) architecture in such grand detail that you are prepared to run off and write your own provider package. The goal is to provide you with enough insight into the architecture that you as a developer have a rudimentary understanding of how the JCA architecture operates. More precisely, by having an understanding of the SPI architecture, and in particular the factory method design, you will have a higher degree of comfort with the factory methods and thus be able to fully exploit the power of the architecture exposed by the engine classes.

Factory design patterns are simple in concept and provide virtually unlimited extensibility, and it is the underpinnings of this design pattern that give the JCA architecture (and by extension the JCE) its true power. Each core JCA engine is located in the java.security package, and it is represented by an abstract class (e.g., MessageDigest represents a message digest engine) that extends another abstract class with an identical name and an appended suffix of "Spi" (e.g., MessageDigestSpi). When a provider writes a cryptographic function, they must determine the engine through which their function will be exposed. For example, if we were to write a new and improved message digest, it would ultimately need to be accessible via one of the factory methods on the MessageDigest engine.

> NOTE: Developers work exclusively through the engine and never directly access either an SPI class or a concrete implementation by name. In fact, the Java language helps ensure this because the SPI class and the engine class are declared as abstract, ensuring neither can be directly instantiated.

The factory methods on the engines are easy to identify. They use a well-known factory method naming pattern, getInstance(String algorithm). When invoked, the method locates (and if necessary instantiates) a concrete class suitable for the request. Recall that the physical implementations *extend* the engine class (e.g., public class MyMessageDigest extends MessageDigest), and the invocation of the factory method casts the instance back to its ancestor class (e.g., `return (MessageDigest) new MyMessageDigest())`. Let's revisit one of the code examples from earlier:

```
MessageDigest md5 = MessageDigest.getInstance("MD5");
```

The invocation of this one line of code provides us with a concrete implementation of a message digest that implements the MD5 algorithm. Fundamentally, we have no idea on the surface which provider the JCA is using to fulfill this request, nor do we really care. As we get into more detailed code examples later in the text, proper exception handling will be introduced to handle situations where the named algorithm is not available.

> NOTE: Throughout the rest of this book we will use the phrase *standard pair of engine factory methods* to represent the two most prevalent factory methods found on nearly every engine, `getInstance(algorithm)` and `getInstance(algorithm, provider)`. This keeps us from having to repeatedly redefine identical method signatures and method operation for each engine covered.

1.5 Installing Providers

The role of a provider in Java's cryptography platform is very important. Sun isn't in the business of developing cryptographic algorithms. It's really that simple. This is not intended as a slam against Sun; on the contrary, it is a credit to them for encouraging the cryptographic researchers to design, build, and publish their implementations through a provider. Almost every application with strong cryptography needs will deploy with it one or more third party JCE providers.

As previously stated, each provider includes implementations of one or more cryptographic algorithms that may be software-only or hardware/software combinations—all of which is encapsulated behind the JCA's engine metaphor. Knowing how to access additional providers is an important ability every developer should understand. In fact, developers can access provider implementations using one of two possible strategies.

- *Opaque algorithm strategy* is where the developer simply requests an algorithm by name, allowing the JCA to choose a provider based on set of rules covered shortly. Think of the opaque algorithm strategy as a black box—developers have no idea what goes on inside the box, just the end result of receiving an instance of the engine class that implements the requested algorithm.

- *Transparent algorithm strategy* is where the developer explicitly names the algorithm and the provider that must supply the implementation of that algorithm. This approach effectively side-steps several of the JCA design goals, and it should only be used in rare situations. The transparency is related to the fact that you can see inside of the algorithm, that is, who it is from, how it is implemented, unique idiosyncrasies as a result of this provider's implementation, etc.

Providers can be registered either statically or dynamically, and the exact approach used will be determined based on the application's nature, runtime environment, and deployment method. For example, if you control the JRE static may make more sense, but if your software will be deployed to heterogeneous environments, a dynamic approach may be the simplest in terms of configuration.

1.5.1   Static Provider Registration

Static registration of a provider occurs through a formal declaration process in the Java Runtime Environment. Sun's documentation on this topic is included under the *Installing Providers* section of the JCA JavaDocs [1]. Specifically, the Sun JDK 1.4 statically registers providers in the file found at $JAVA_HOME/jre/lib/security/java.security. The java.security file allows individual end-users to establish a preferred search sequence. When the developer opts to use an opaque algorithm strategy, the providers are searched sequentially until a match is found. The search sequence relies on the name-value pair naming convention commonly used by Java properties files. For example, my java.security file declares its providers in this sequence:

```
security.provider.1=sun.security.provider.Sun

security.provider.2=com.sun.net.ssl.internal.ssl.Provider

security.provider.3=com.sun.rsajca.Provider

security.provider.4=org.bouncycastle.jce.provider.BouncyCastleProvider

security.provider.5=sun.security.jgss.SunProvider
```

The numbers 1 ... 5 represent the explicit search sequence. This list is strict in that the providers must be in counting order (e.g., 1,2,3,4 ... and not 4,1,3,2 ...), and a number cannot be skipped. The opaque algorithm strategy queries each provider to determine if they support a concrete implementation of the algorithm requested by the developer. The first provider that can respond "yes" will always service the request when an opaque algorithm strategy is employed. Notice that each provider entry listed is identified with a fully qualified package name.

While this step formally introduces what is effectively a bootstrap routine that registers the provider's offerings, there is still the problem of exposing the physical classes. Providers will typically ship production code inside of a signed .jar file, and there are two ways in which these classes can be added to a runtime environment.

Provider Class Deployment: Option 1

The first option is to drop the .jar file into the $JAVA_HOME/jre/lib/ext directory. This approach effectively treats the .jar as an extension of the physical runtime environment. Any .jar file dropped here will be found prior to classes accessible to the system class loader. This option makes the provider's implementation available to all applications, there is no messing around with the $CLASSPATH environment variable, and with mini-mal legwork, you can validate the signature of the .jar prior to blindly placing it into the extensions directory.

If you need a refresher on class loaders, one of the better discussions on Java's class loader architecture is from JavaGeeks.com [2]. If you haven't had a need to work with Java extensions, you may want to review the Java Extensions FAQ [3].

Provider Class Deployment: Option 2

The alternative to using the extensions directory is to manually add the provider's .jar file onto the $CLASSPATH environment variable.

1.5.2 Dynamic Provider Registration

Dynamic registration is possible and often more convenient than static registration. Explicit privileges still have to be declared for the provider before the attempted dynamic registration when a SecurityManager is in effect. Specifically (using the example from the Java Cryptography Extension documentation), if the *MyJCE* provider deploys their perti-nent classes in the *MyApp.jar* file that is copied to your */localWork* directory, a grant like this would be required if you were using a SecurityManager.

```
grant codeBase "file:/localWork/MyApp.jar" {

        Permission java.security.SecurityPermission

                "insertProvider.MyJCE";

};
```

The code examples in this book that require the use of a third party provider will use dynamic registration, and no SecurityManager is assumed. Deployment of the physical JCE provider class files is a manual process that you will have to complete, and either of the two deployment options described here will be adequate.

NOTE: Despite these well-documented procedures for accessing a provider, there are numer-ous posts throughout the web detailing how custom class loaders (especially poorly written ones) do not properly recognize an installed provider. The fact is that each IDE, EJB, and Servlet container on the market uses a distinct architecture that will have its own set of idiosyncrasies. Be sure to check with your vendor for any special considerations you may need to be aware of when accessing the JCE, or more specifically third party providers, from inside these environments.

When attempting to dynamically register a JCE provider, that provider cannot be registered too high up in the search order due to a bug in the Sun JVM. This bug has been duplicated on both Mac OS X and Windows 2000, XP. It was registered with Apple as Java Bug #3294108

(JCE Providers Crash with Bus Error) and with Sun's Java Developer Connection under JDC Review ID 188804 (Dynamic Registration of JCE Provider in Position 1 Results in Stack Overflow). If your code is going to employ a dynamic registration strategy, do not place your JCE provider of choice in position 1 without checking if Sun has closed this bug first! Here is the stack trace that results:

```
java.lang.StackOverflowError
    at java.lang.ClassNotFoundException.<init>(ClassNotFoundException.java:65)
    at java.lang.ClassLoader.findBootstrapClass(Native Method)
    at java.lang.ClassLoader.findBootstrapClass0(ClassLoader.java:723)
    at java.lang.ClassLoader.loadClass(ClassLoader.java:294)
    at java.lang.ClassLoader.loadClass(ClassLoader.java:292)
    at sun.misc.Launcher$AppClassLoader.loadClass(Launcher.java:265)
    at java.lang.ClassLoader.loadClass(ClassLoader.java:255)
    at java.security.Security.doGetImpl(Security.java:1122)
    at java.security.Security.doGetImpl(Security.java:1083)
    at java.security.Security.getImpl(Security.java:1044)
    at java.security.MessageDigest.getInstance(MessageDigest.java:120)
    at sun.security.util.ManifestEntryVerifier.setEntry
        (ManifestEntryVerifier.java:111)
    at java.util.jar.JarVerifier.beginEntry(JarVerifier.java:151)
    at java.util.jar.JarVerifier$VerifierStream.<init>(JarVerifier.java:352)
    at java.util.jar.JarFile.getInputStream(JarFile.java:323)
    at sun.misc.URLClassPath$5.getInputStream(URLClassPath.java:617)
    at sun.misc.Resource.getBytes(Resource.java:57)
```

To give you insight into what appears to be happening, when you dynamically register a new JCE provider, the .jar must be verified. A cycle ensues—the MessageDigest engine must be used to verify the .jar, but because the logic expects to use the default provider, which is now the new provider, it must verify the .jar and around it goes until a stack overflow occurs. It would appear that the engine, if being used to verify a .jar file, should explicitly request the SUN provider. Nothing in the java.security file gives any indication that a provider cannot be placed into position 1 dynamically:

```
# There must be at least one provider specification in java.security.
# There is a default provider that comes standard with the JDK. It
```

```
# is called the "SUN" provider, and its Provider subclass
# named Sun appears in the sun.security.provider package. Thus, the
# "SUN" provider is registered via the following:
#
# security.provider.1=sun.security.provider.Sun
#
# (The number 1 is used for the default provider.)
#
# Note: Statically registered Provider subclasses are instantiated
# when the system is initialized. Providers can be dynamically
# registered instead by calls to either the addProvider or
# insertProviderAt method in the Security class.
```

However, clearly there are some dependencies on the base algorithms from the SUN provider that require it to always be in position 1. For our purposes in this book, I arbitrarily registered my providers dynamically after position 5; your environment may require adjustment of this number up or down.

1.6 JCA Helper Classes

Understanding the provider architecture is important, and it is equally important to understand a couple of the utility or helper classes. The two classes we will look at include the java.security.Security and the java.security.Provider. These classes in tandem can provide access to JCA/JCE metadata, actually perform the dynamic installation of a provider, etc. The remainder of this chapter builds on our architectural understanding, presenting practical code examples and discussions around JCA metadata and providers.

1.6.1 The Security Class

The java.security.Security class is directly responsible for provider management. There is no public constructor, so its functionality is accessed only via its publicly declared static methods. This class also enjoys a strong working relationship with the Java security policies, as defined in $JAVA_HOME/jre/lib/security/java.policy. For example, this file reinforces our earlier statements surrounding the extensions loader and dynamic registration of a provider.

```
// Standard extensions get all permissions by default

grant codeBase "file:${java.home}/lib/ext/*" {

        permission java.security.AllPermission;

};
```

This grant indicates that any .jar file loaded from the $JAVA_HOME/jre/lib/ext directory has full permissions to do what they see fit.

There are two ways to dynamically register a third-party JCE provider programmatically if editing the $JAVA_HOME/jre/lib/security/java.security file on client machines is considered non-trivial. The Security class declares two methods, addProvider() and insertProviderAt() that append the provider to the end of the list and at a 1-based position, respectively. In addition to these registration methods, there is a very useful method for data mining—getProviders(). This method is rarely invoked directly by the developer; it returns an array of Provider objects. The best way to understand how these two classes (Security and Provider) complement each other is through code examples. Let's walk through the Provider class and those examples next.

1.6.2   The Provider Class

The java.security.Provider class serves two primary purposes: accessing provider metadata and registering implementations of cryptographic services. On the surface, this information may seem trivial to the developer, and in fact, developers will probably have little to no *direct* interaction with this class. However, to the provider, this class represents the cornerstone of development. Each provider *must* subclass the Provider class, and their constructor must provide values for mandatory metadata fields, including but not limited to the provider name, version number, and a list of name-value pairs that define what concrete implementations the provider supports.

To verify that each provider's class extends the Provider class, jump out to a command line and use the javap (as a mnemonic aid, think of javap as Java "Ping" or Java "Print" where details about the class is displayed) command:

```
wiseman in ~ (2)--> javap sun.security.provider.Sun

Compiled from Sun.java

public final class sun.security.provider.Sun extends java.security.Provider {

        public sun.security.provider.Sun();

}
```

This output verifies that the sun.security.provider.Sun class correctly extends the java.security.Provider class. It also indicates that the provider's class does not expose any additional methods beyond that declared in the Provider class. The question at hand is how to determine the programmatic name of any given provider's implementation. Let's take a look how to decipher that information.

1.6.3 Code Example: Obtaining a List of Installed Providers, Formal Names

The core class java.security.Security class is used to obtain a list of providers. This list is represented as an array of java.security.Provider classes. It is imperative that developers remember there is a difference between the logical and physical names of the providers. By that I mean that the provider may be commonly referred to in speech as the "Bouncy Castle" provider, yet in terms of using a transparent algorithm strategy the provider parameter that must be used is "BC" or a NoSuchProviderException will be thrown.

> NOTE: Whenever a transparent algorithm strategy is employed, always explicitly catch the NoSuchProviderException and handle it effectively!

When developers use an opaque algorithm strategy, they expressly rely on the declared order of the providers in the java.security properties class found inside the JRE. The invocation of any getInstance(algorithmName) factory method delegates the provider selection to the JRE, or more specifically its java.security properties file and the order in which providers are listed—this includes any dynamically registered providers and their respective priority. When developers determine that a specific provider's implementation offers desirable characteristics, they may choose to switch to a transparent strategy and explicitly name the provider. In this situation, the invocation of any getInstance(algorithmName, providerName) factory method explicitly locates the provider's class. Where does the provider name come from? Recall that each provider must declare a formal provider name as part of the subclassed Provider constructor. The following example is extremely useful for quickly printing out a list of the available providers and their programmatic provider name:

Example 1.2 Sample Code Location: com.mkp.jce.chap1.ProviderDetail

```
try
{

        //Dynamically register our Cryptix provider

        //without requiring java.security modification

        //Place the provider in the fifth position

        Provider prov = new cryptix.jce.provider.CryptixCrypto();

        Security.insertProviderAt(prov, 5);


        if("all".equalsIgnoreCase(args[0]))
        {
```

```java
Provider[] providers = Security.getProviders();
for(int i=0;i<providers.length;i++)
{
        System.out.println("********************");
        System.out.println("** Provider: " +
                providers[i].getName());
        System.out.println("********************");
        System.out.print(providers[i].toString());
        System.out.print(" is formally referred to as '" +
                providers[i].getName() + "'");

        System.out.println(" in a getInstance() factory method");
        System.out.println("");
}
        System.out.println("Total Providers: "+providers.length);


} else
{
        Provider provider = Security.getProvider(args[0]);
        System.out.println(provider.getName() +
                " formally supports: ");

        Iterator iter = provider.entrySet().iterator();
        while(iter.hasNext())
        {
                Map.Entry entry = (Map.Entry) iter.next();
                System.out.println("\t" + entry.getKey() + " = " +
                        entry.getValue());
        }
}
```

```
} catch (NullPointerException nspe)
{

      //NPE means Provider wasn't found!

      System.err.println("The requested provider is not installed in the JRE");
} catch (ArrayIndexOutOfBoundsException aioobe)
{

      System.err.println("Usage: java ProviderDetail providerName");

      System.err.println("Set providerName to 'all' to list all");

}
```

Here is the output of this example from my machine using "all" as the command line argument:

```
********************

** Provider: SUN

********************

SUN version 1.2 is formally referred to as the 'SUN' provider in a

getInstance() factory method


********************

** Provider: SunJSSE

********************

SunJSSE version 1.41 is formally referred to as the 'SunJSSE' provider in a

getInstance() factory method


********************

** Provider: SunRsaSign

********************

SunRsaSign version 1.0 is formally referred to as the 'SunRsaSign' provider in

a getInstance() factory method
```

```
********************
** Provider: SunJCE
********************
```

SunJCE version 1.4 is formally referred to as the 'SunJCE' provider in a getInstance() factory method

```
********************
** Provider: BC
********************
```

BC version 1.19 is formally referred to as the 'BC' provider in a getInstance() factory method

```
********************
** Provider: CryptixCrypto
********************
```

CryptixCrypto version 1.3 is formally referred to as the 'CryptixCrypto' provider in a getInstance() factory method

```
********************
** Provider: SunJGSS
********************
```

SunJGSS version 1.0 is formally referred to as the 'SunJGSS' provider in a getInstance() factory method

Total Providers: 7

The com.mkp.jce.misc.CryptoUtils class provided in the code examples offers a useful method that makes it easy for your applications to determine if a specific provider is available. The signature looks like this:

```
public final static boolean providerExists(String providerName);
```

This helper method can be used to eliminate NoSuchProviderException risks at run time.

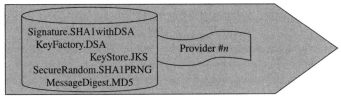

Java Cryptography Architecture

Figure 1.2: Providers define one or more engine implementations.

The other cited purpose for the Provider class is to present the JCA with a list of concrete implementations that each provider offers. Let's see what the code looks like to find out this information.

1.6.4 Code Example: Listing a Provider's Supported Algorithms

The Provider class defines an un-modifiable view into the engine algorithms that the provider supports, as depicted in Figure 1.2. This is inline with the notion that the Provider class is strictly about metadata, and supports our statement that developers will rarely directly interact with one of the Provider subclasses. We've already described the search preference for providers that is used when an engine's getInstance() factory method is invoked. As the factory method iterates over the providers in their preferred search sequence, each Provider implementation is queried to determine if it has implemented the requested algorithm.

Conceptually, the lookup is very simple. The Provider class declares an entrySet() method that returns a java.util.Set of Map.Entry objects. Each Map.Entry object contains a name-value pair that represents either a concrete implementation or an aliased name that points to a concrete implementation. For example, let's say that we invoked the following Signature engine factory method:

```
Signature mySignature = Signature.getInstance("SHA1withDSA");
```

The argument indicates that we are requesting a SHA-1 with DSA signature algorithm. We also are using an opaque algorithm strategy, so each provider will be searched in the order defined by the java.security file—taking into consideration any dynamically registered providers and their requested priority. Using the same java.security file documented earlier in this chapter (and assuming no dynamically registered providers exist), we see that the SUN provider is first in our list. Let's see what algorithms this provider supports.

Example 1.3 Sample Code Location: com.mkp.jce.chap1.DisorganizedListing

```
try
{

        //Lookup the named provider using its formal name
        Provider provider = Security.getProvider(args[0]);

        System.out.print(provider.getName());
        System.out.println(" formally supports the following algorithms:");

        //Step over the list of supported algorithms
        Iterator iter = provider.entrySet().iterator();
        while(iter.hasNext())
        {
                Map.Entry entry = (Map.Entry) iter.next();
                System.out.println("\t" +
                        entry.getKey() + " = " + entry.getValue());
        }
} catch (NullPointerException nspe)
{

        //NPE means Provider wasn't found!
        System.err.println("The provider you requested is not installed in the
JRE");
} catch (ArrayIndexOutOfBoundsException aioobe)
{

        System.err.println("Usage: java ProviderDetail providerName");
}
```

Running this code example produces the following abbreviated output. Notice in particular the three bold lines that relate to our SHA-1 with DSA request:

```
wiseman in ~/src/jce (11)--> java com.mkp.jce.chap1.DisorganizedListing SUN

        Alg.Alias.KeyFactory.1.2.840.10040.4.1 = DSA
```

```
Alg.Alias.Signature.1.2.840.10040.4.3 = SHA1withDSA

Alg.Alias.KeyPairGenerator.OID.1.2.840.10040.4.1 = DSA

CertStore.LDAP LDAPSchema = RFC2587
```

Signature.SHA1withDSA KeySize = 1024

Signature.SHA1withDSA ImplementedIn = Software

```
CertPathValidator.PKIX ValidationAlgorithm = draft-ietf-pkix-new-part1-
   08.txt

CertPathBuilder.PKIX = sun.security.provider.certpath.SunCertPathBuilder

Alg.Alias.KeyFactory.1.3.14.3.2.12 = DSA

CertStore.LDAP = sun.security.provider.certpath.LDAPCertStore

AlgorithmParameterGenerator.DSA =
   sun.security.provider.DSAParameterGenerator

Alg.Alias.KeyPairGenerator.1.3.14.3.2.12 = DSA

Alg.Alias.Signature.SHA/DSA = SHA1withDSA

Alg.Alias.Signature.1.3.14.3.2.13 = SHA1withDSA

SecureRandom.SHA1PRNG = sun.security.provider.SecureRandom

Alg.Alias.Signature.DSS = SHA1withDSA

CertStore.Collection =
   sun.security.provider.certpath.CollectionCertStore

KeyFactory.DSA ImplementedIn = Software

KeyStore.JKS ImplementedIn = Software
```

Signature.SHA1withDSA = sun.security.provider.DSA

```
MessageDigest.SHA ImplementedIn = Software
```

Based on this information, the factory method of the Signature engine is able to effectively determine the following four items from the SUN provider:

1. The SUN provider offers an implementation of the SHA1withDSA algorithm
2. The actual class that implements the algorithm can be found in sun.security. provider.DSA. This can be verified through a javap command on the command line which shows that the class extends the java.security.Signature class

3. The implementation in question is software (as opposed to hardware) based; for example, some type of cryptographic device attached to a serial or USB port)

4. The implementation uses a key that is 1024 bits in size.

Also of interest in this file is the use of a string naming convention that allows quick lookups without iterating over every key. With the exception of the Alg.Alias prefix (which is a special case for aliasing algorithms that go by many different names), the prefix prior to the first '.' in the key name equates to the type of engine, and the suffix after the first '.' in the key name corresponds with the proper algorithm name. Using this notation, the Signature factory method—as well as any engine's factory method—can quickly and effectively determine if a provider implements the requested algorithm. Using the read-only metadata stored in the Set, the factory method simply looks for the pattern "<EngineType>.<AlgorithmName>" and if found, the algorithm is supported and the value of that key is the name of the concrete class that implements the algorithm. The factory then creates an instance of the class (usually through a Class.forName() lookup-instantiation design) and returns it, which the JVM will automatically cast to the appropriate engine type. If we wanted to determine if a provider supported an MD5 message digest, the Message Digest engine's factory method simply looks up each provider (if not explicitly named) and attempts to locate a key named MessageDigest.MD5 in the metadata.

1.6.5   Code Example: Obtaining a List of Installed Algorithms

Perhaps one of the most common questions fielded from new JCE developers is how to determine what algorithms are installed, or more specifically, what are the formal names of the installed algorithms. There are two different techniques for obtaining this information, and both key off of the formal engine name, for example, Signature or Message Digest or Cipher. The first technique is via the Security class. It declares an elementary java.util.Set getAlgorithms(String engineName) method. Iterate over the set and you see the proper names for each algorithm registered with the engine.

Example 1.4 Sample Code Location: com.mkp.jce.chap1.SimpleEngineListing

```
//Dynamically register our Cryptix provider

//without requiring java.security modification

//Place the provider in the fifth position

//Provider prov = new cryptix.jce.provider.CryptixCrypto();

//Security.insertProviderAt(prov, 5);


Set set = Security.getAlgorithms(args[0]);

Iterator iter = set.iterator();
```

```
while(iter.hasNext())
{
    System.out.println(iter.next().toString());
}
```

This small code sample produces algorithm names that can be effectively used in an opaque provider strategy. Nothing about the provider that implements the algorithm is revealed—the algorithm essentially remains a black box.

This code sample also demonstrates the use of the Security class to dynamically register new JCE providers. Running the code with the dynamic registration commented out should reveal a small list similar to this for the Signature engine:

```
MD2WITHRSA

SHA1WITHRSA

SHA1WITHDSA

MD5WITHRSA
```

Now, if we uncomment the two lines of code that dynamically register the Cryptix provider, we should see a much larger list of algorithms that the Signature engine supports.

```
MD2WITHRSA

RIPEMD128WITHRSA

SHA/DSA

SHA-384/RSA/PKCS#1

SHA1WITHRSA

SHA1WITHDSA

RSASSA-PSS/SHA-1

RSASSA-PSS/SHA-512

RSASSA-PSS/SHA-384

RSASSA-PSS/SHA-256

RIPEMD160WITHRSA

SHA-256/RSA/PKCS#1

MD5WITHRSA

SHA-512/RSA/PKCS#1
```

RAWDSA

MD4WITHRSA

The other technique for locating the nomenclature of the installed algorithms is via the Provider class. Let's see an example of this approach:

Example 1.5 Sample Code Location: com.mkp.jce.chap1.CompleteEngineListing

```
try
{
        //Dynamically register our Cryptix provider
        //without requiring java.security modification
        //Place the provider in the first position
        Provider prov = new cryptix.jce.provider.CryptixCrypto();
        Security.insertProviderAt(prov, 1);


        Provider provider = Security.getProvider(args[0]);
        System.out.println(provider.getName() + " - " + args[1] + " engine :\n");


        EngineIterator iter = new EngineIterator(provider, args[1]);
        while(iter.hasNext())
        {
                Map.Entry entry = (Map.Entry) iter.next();
                if(!iter.isAlias())
                {
                        _description =
                                entry.getKey().toString().substring(1 +
                                args[1].length()) + " as implemented in class " +
                                entry.getValue().toString();
                } else
                {
                        _description =
                                entry.getValue().toString() + " is also aliased as" +
```

```
                        entry.getKey().toString().substring(
                                EngineIterator.ALGORITHM_ALIAS.length() +
                                args[1].length() + 1);
                }


                //Add our description to our sorted list
                _sortedListing.add(_description);
        }


        Iterator printIter = _sortedListing.iterator();
        while(printIter.hasNext())
        {
                System.out.println(printIter.next().toString());
        }

} catch (ArrayIndexOutOfBoundsException aioobe)
{
        System.err.println("Usage: java EngineListing providerName engineType");
        System.err.println("Engine names are case-sensitive");
}
```

This example uses a utility class I threw together called EngineIterator. It essentially is a class that implements the java.util.Iterator interface, and provides some logic for skipping over the extraneous entries from engines we aren't interested in viewing. This isn't a book on the Java Collections, so we'll treat the EngineIterator as a black box utility class. Running this code for the CryptixCrypto provider, Signature engine reveals the following output:

```
CryptixCrypto formally supports the following implementations for the Signature
    engine :

MD2withRSA as implemented in class
    cryptix.jce.provider.rsa.RSASignature_PKCS1_MD2
```

```
MD2withRSA is also
  aliased to the name MD2/RSA/PKCS#1
```
MD4withRSA as implemented in class
  cryptix.jce.provider.rsa.RSASignature_PKCS1_MD4
MD4withRSA is also aliased to the name MD4/RSA/PKCS#1
```
MD5withRSA as implemented in class
  cryptix.jce.provider.rsa.RSASignature_PKCS1_MD5
MD5withRSA is also aliased to the name MD5/RSA/PKCS#1
RIPEMD128withRSA as implemented in class
cryptix.jce.provider.rsa.RSASignature_PKCS1_RIPEMD128
RIPEMD128withRSA is also aliased to the name RIPEMD-128/RSA/PKCS#1
RIPEMD160withRSA as implemented in class
  cryptix.jce.provider.rsa.RSASignature_PKCS1_RIPEMD160
RIPEMD160withRSA is also aliased to the name RIPEMD-160/RSA/PKCS#1
RSASSA-PSS/SHA-1 as implemented in class
  cryptix.jce.provider.rsa.RSASignature_PSS_SHA1
RSASSA-PSS/SHA-256 as implemented in class
cryptix.jce.provider.rsa.RSASignature_PSS_SHA256
RSASSA-PSS/SHA-384 as implemented in class
cryptix.jce.provider.rsa.RSASignature_PSS_SHA384
RSASSA-PSS/SHA-512 as implemented in class
cryptix.jce.provider.rsa.RSASignature_PSS_SHA512
RawDSA as implemented in class cryptix.jce.provider.dsa.RawDSASignature
SHA-256/RSA/PKCS#1 as implemented in class
cryptix.jce.provider.rsa.RSASignature_PKCS1_SHA256
SHA-384/RSA/PKCS#1 as implemented in class
cryptix.jce.provider.rsa.RSASignature_PKCS1_SHA384
SHA-512/RSA/PKCS#1 as implemented in class
cryptix.jce.provider.rsa.RSASignature_PKCS1_SHA512
SHA/DSA as implemented in class cryptix.jce.provider.dsa.DSASignature
```

SHA1withRSA as implemented in class

  cryptix.jce.provider.rsa.RSASignature_PKCS1_SHA1

SHA1withRSA is also aliased to the name SHA-1/RSA/PKCS#1

The generated output provides further insight into how the JCE architecture supports many common names for a single algorithm. All of the Alg.Alias entries we saw when we ran the DisorganizedListing for the SUN provider should now make sense after seeing this example. Take a look at the MD4withRSA signature. Let's look at what happens when this one line of code is invoked:

```
Signature signature = Signature.getInstance("MD4withRSA");
```

When the Signature engine's factory method receives a request to provide a class that implements the MD4withRSA algorithm, it searches through the provider's in their registered prioritized sequence. When it finds a provider that offers a solution to this request, the engine grabs the fully qualified class name (it is implemented in a concrete class cryptix.jce.provider.rsa.RSASignature_PKCS1_MD4) and issues a Class.forName() to load the implementing class. Contractually via the SPI, this class extends the Signature class, and after an instance of it is created, it is returned (cast to its ancestor, the Signature class) from the call. What our listing demonstrates is that the following two lines of code accomplish the same thing, instantiating an identical class:

```
Signature signature = Signature.getInstance("MD4withRSA");

Signature signature = Signature.getInstance("MD4/RSA/PKCS#1");
```

As we can see, the architecture is extremely robust, allowing each algorithm to expose itself under any number of different names. However, this "feature" is really a double-edged sword. The JCA fails to define a formal algorithm namespace. The implication of this missing namespace is best conveyed through an example. Imagine two third party providers A and B are installed in that order. Provider A may implement an algorithm for use in the MessageDigest engine with a name of "MD-5" while provider B may implement an identical algorithm, but name it "MD5" instead. The algorithm names are strings arbitrarily chosen by the provider! If a developer requests an "MD5" algorithm from the engine, provider A won't be considered because it doesn't implement an "MD5" algorithm. As a result, it puts an undue burden on both providers and developers. Providers are forced to alias out each of their implementations with many common names to ensure they get adequate consideration during an algorithm search, and developers struggle with an ever-growing combination of arbitrary names from providers.

1.7 Working with Jurisdiction Policy Files

Most of us write applications that are run internally throughout the corporate environment. However, some of us find ourselves in the unique position of writing applications that are going to be exported. Unfortunately developers are not immune from the political lines drawn on a map, and, as a result, some care must be taken to ensure laws are not broken if the software is going to be exported. This section is aimed squarely at those developing commercial software applications that are going to be exported. Ironically, the problem may not necessarily reside with the exporting country but rather the importing country.

By default, the JDK 1.4 jurisdiction policy files support what is known as "strong but limited" cryptography. An "unlimited strength" policy file is available for download from http://java.sun.com for those living in eligible countries. The JCE will enforce this policy file, limiting things like the maximum key size that a cipher can use when encrypting. There isn't much value in reprinting the process one goes through to deliver an "exempt" application. For more information, grab a copy of the JCE documentation [5] and review "How to Make Applications 'Exempt' from Cryptographic Restrictions" and the sections that follow it.

## chapter 2

Working with Symmetric Ciphers

We now have a strong understanding of how the JCA/JCE provide the necessary infrastructure to support cryptographic operations in Java. With this information in hand, we are ready to build our knowledge base and begin to explore the world of symmetric ciphers. The first code example in this book (SimpleExample from Chapter 1) demonstrated a symmetric cipher in use. At the end of this chapter, you will be reading and writing code similar to that example.

A **Symmetric Cipher** is depicted in Figure 2.1. The symmetric cipher is an engine that transforms **plaintext** into **ciphertext** through the use of a **secret key**. Plaintext is a message in its native form; you and I could simply look at it and read it. Ciphertext is the result of the encryption operation, and it should appear as an incomprehensible flow of bytes. The secret key is the critical piece in the system; if the secret key is compromised, then so is the message hidden in the ciphertext. The secret key used to generate the ciphertext is the same secret key used to decipher and return the original plaintext. More specifically, the sender and receiver both use the same secret key.

Often people interchange the words cipher and code, but there is a fundamental difference. A code creates a substitute for an entire word or phrase; for example, from this point forward Billy will be known as "Fortune Cookie." This is substantially different than a cipher that will operate against (for example) one byte at a time, yielding an incomprehensible sequence of bytes completely different from the original.

The goal of a cipher is to protect the information by making the ciphertext either too expensive to decrypt (e.g., having to purchase 10,000 super computers and develop software to coordinate a brute force attack in parallel) or so outdated by the time the ciphertext is cracked the information is worthless or a statement of the obvious. To protect the information, it is imperative that a strong secret key be fed into the symmetric cipher. People make terrible choices when it comes to generating secret keys. With few exceptions,

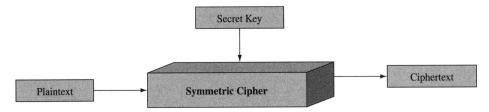

Figure 2.1: Architecture of a symmetric cipher.

most of us would have a hard time remembering a large 20, 30, or 40 character random password. Overall, we have a tendency to pick secret keys (often referred to as *passwords*) that are short and easy to remember. *secret god dev scott dba admin* All of these are terrible examples of common passwords used in production systems.

Symmetric ciphers play an important role in cryptography today. Symmetric ciphers are fast and capable of performing encryption operations even when the input data is very large. Some symmetric cipher algorithms lend themselves to parallel encryption operations that can take full advantage of multiple CPUs.

Symmetric ciphers and nearly every other aspect of cryptography require reliable random number generation capabilities. A collection of random numbers is then used as the secret key. Random here means *pure* random data, like measuring the vibration of the earth or sampling weather related data. The random numbers generated by something like the Solitaire card game on your PC is not suitable for use in cryptography because patterns often form. Perhaps you've seen the cards dealt out in similar patterns. A pattern is not random; it is reproducible, and thus a very poor source for generating a random secret key. Reproducible is bad because it increases the odds that someone else might reproduce the same sequence and use it to decipher sensitive data. Before we take a close look at symmetric cipher operations via the JCE, we're going to review the random number generation capabilities defined by the JCA.

2.1   Random Number Generation

Sadly, there is no easy way to hook up our computer to sample earth vibrations or something similar. Research into the generation of random numbers using computers and software continues today. It is easy to find on almost every platform the presence of a *cryptographically secure pseudo-random number generator*, or **CSPRNG** for short. Kerckhoff's Principle[25] tells us that the secrecy must reside in the secret key, not in the algorithm. In essence, always assume that the cryptanalyst trying to break your ciphertext has obtained the complete details of the employed cipher.

Ciphertext is only as strong as the secret key used to lock the message. The **key space** relates to the number of possible key combinations that could be used by a given encryption algorithm. For example, a 40-bit key space means that there are 2^{40} possible keys. Similar, a 128-bit key space means that there are 2^{128} possible key combinations. While the difference may seem minimal on the surface, increases in key space truly carry exponential differences. Modern supercomputers could use a **brute force attack** (try each key in sequence) to break a 40-bit key in well under a day, however, that same supercomputer could spend years and years attempting a brute force attack on a 128-bit key and not find the solution. By the time the key was found, presumably the value of the information encrypted has become meaningless.

How long is the password that you used to log in to your computer this morning? A case-*sensitive* alphanumeric key space contains a mere 62 characters ([A...Z], [a...z], [0...9]). As an example, let's say that your password is 6 characters long, like S*n00py*. Without dropping into too much math theory, suffice to say that the total possible alphanumeric combinations are represented by 62*62*62*62*62*62, where each character could be any one of the available 62 characters. That's a mere 56,800,235,584 possible keys. On the surface, it appears to provide a great deal of security—56 billion possible keys. We live in a world where a dual-CPU machine running with a clock speed in excess of 3 GHz is readily available. That 6 character password has an effective bit size of 35-bits. Without any empirical data, let's assume that a machine like that just described is running Linux, and it could attempt 500,000 guesses per minute. The entire 6-byte alphanumeric key space could be searched in a brute force decryption attempt in less than 32 hours. Do you still think your 56 billion combinations represent a significant deterrent to someone who really wants to crack your password? I don't.

The fact is that strength of a key is directly proportional to the size of the key and its randomness. Data that are going to be stored for extended periods of time (like data found inside of a database) should use a larger, more random key to help better protect the data from a brute force attack that might occur over a long period of time. So how do we generate such a strong secret key? Well, the JCA includes a SecureRandom engine explicitly for such purposes.

2.2 **The** SecureRandom **Engine**

The ability to build cryptographically secure pseudo-random number generators (CSPRNG) is crucial. To meet this demand, the JCA includes an engine capable of serving up CSPRNG algorithms. True to its engine form, it implements the standard pair of engine factory methods, for example:

```
SecureRandom csprng = SecureRandom.getInstance("SHA1PRNG");
```

Actual random number generation cannot occur until after the engine initializes its internal state, known as *establishing a seed value*. Think of the seed value as the "starting point" of random number generation. Programmatically, you can establish the seed value by invoking the setSeed(long seed) method immediately after obtaining the CSPRNG instance from the factory method:

```
csprng.setSeed(31592712351); //Fingers Pounding Keyboard Number
```

Extracting random bytes from the CSPRNG is done with a call to the nextBytes(byte[] output) method. The larger the byte[] passed to the method, the more random bytes the CSPRNG yields.

Of particular noteworthiness is that additional calls to the setSeed(long seed) method *after* extracting one or more random byte arrays operate in a *supplemental* nature. In other words, the original seed value is not replaced; attempting to ensure that repeated calls avoid deterministic sequences (patterns) in the generated random values. A deterministic algorithm is an algorithm with no elements of chance, where the result is well determined and nonrandom[6]. Thus, a deterministic algorithm is *not* well suited for our cryptographic activities because an attacker could potentially determine the sequence of bytes used in the secret key.

It is worth noting that the java.lang.Math class contains a random() method. This method is **not** suitable for cryptographic operations because it uses a deterministic algorithm. The JavaDocs on the function indicate that the pseudo-random values are uniformly distributed between 0.0 and 1.0. True randomness is never uniformly distributed. The speed at which someone types on a keyboard over a period of time, the vibrations of a building as traffic rushes by—each of these are truly random and not uniform in nature. Uniformity only helps strengthen the position of the crypanalyst. Those interested in reading more about the generation of random numbers and nondeterministic algorithms should review the classic work on the topic—Donald Knuth's *The Art of Computer Programming, Volume 2*, (Boston: Addison-Wesley, 1997) Chapter 3, "Random Numbers."

2.2.1   Code Example: Generating Random Values

One of the nicest features of the JCA's SecureRandom engine is that it declares a number of helper methods that are used to generate more than just random bytes of data. This subtlety is a result of the JCA architects having the presence to define the SecureRandom engine as extending the java.util.Random class. By itself, the java.util.Random class is **not** suitable for cryptographic operations. However, when it is seeded using the SHA1PRNG (or another nondeterministic algorithm) as the SecureRandom engine does, it becomes acceptable for use in our cryptographic algorithms. The following code example demonstrates this functionality in action, as we generate random boolean, int and byte values:

Example 2.1 Sample Code Location: com.mkp.jce.chap2.CsprngExample

```
1 try
2 {
3      //Locate a SHA1PRNG provider
4      SecureRandom csprng = SecureRandom.getInstance("SHA1PRNG");
5
6      //Generate a randome boolean value
```

```
7        boolean randomBoolean = csprng.nextBoolean();

8

9        //Generate a random int value

10       int randomInt = csprng.nextInt();

11

12        //Generate 3 random bytes

13        byte[3] randomBytes = new byte[3];

14        csprng.nextBytes[randomBytes];

15

16 } catch (NoSuchAlgorithmException e)

17 {

18        //Handle this!

19        e.printStackTrace();

20 }
```

The engine attempts to locate a provider that implements the requested CSPRNG algorithm (SHA1PRNG in this example) on line 4 of the code example. Next, one of two things happens. In our code example, the engine automatically takes the steps necessary to completely randomize its internal state on our first random data request, in this case a call to nextBoolean() on line 7. Alternatively, we could have invoked the setSeed() method at line 5 immediately after locating our SecureRandom instance. This would have told the engine to use our seed instead of generating its own. However, unless you know you have access to a great random seed, it is best to let the engine initialize itself. If we wanted to further seed the engine, at anytime after line 7 we could have invoked one or more setSeed() calls.

Now that we understand how random number sequences suitable for use in cryptographic operations are obtained, we turn our focus towards creating secret keys suitable for use in a symmetric cipher.

2.3 **The** KeyGenerator **Engine**

Every symmetric cipher requires a secret key to perform an encryption operation. As previously stated, the secret key represents the most critical aspect of the symmetric cipher architecture; always assume that the attacker has a full understanding of the symmetric cipher algorithm you are using. The JCA delegates responsibility for symmetric cipher secret key generation to the javax.crypto.KeyGenerator engine class. As an engine, it implements the standard pair of engine factory methods, for example:

```
KeyGenerator kg = KeyGenerator.getInstance("AES");
```

The science of cryptography would be very limited if a cipher algorithm had to be initialized with only a single parameter. In fact, different ciphers use different initialization parameters to implement their functionality. For example, some ciphers may require their secret keys be exactly 56-bits in length, while others may require a minimum key of 128-bits in length. The KeyGenerator engine encapsulates these concepts for us, ultimately creating a data-rich symmetric secret key of appropriate size that contains sufficient initialization data for the named cipher algorithm. The KeyGenerator engine follows the original design goals of the JCA, providing algorithm independent or algorithm specific secret key generation. It does this through a set of overloaded init() methods. You are not required to invoke any of these initialization routines. Instead, you may defer to an algorithm independent initialization based on what the provider deems appropriate, that is, a provider defined default key size generated through a provider defined default source of randomness. Let's look at each scenario in more detail.

2.3.1   Algorithm Independent Initialization

The decision to use algorithm independent initialization may be a result of allowing the application to lookup from a preference file which cipher algorithm it should use at runtime. Each pair of factory methods in the engine accepts String arguments. In Chapter 1, we demonstrated how to inspect the list of available providers and available algorithms each provider defined. It's very realistic to envision an application where the list of providers and cipher algorithms is presented to a power-user, allowing them to make a selection at runtime. This situation would demand the use of an algorithm independent SecretKey initialization. The following init() methods support this approach:

```
init(int keySize)

init(SecureRandom random)

init(int keySize, SecureRandom random)
```

The first init() method specifies the size of the key (the size will be in bits or bytes depending on the cipher algorithm in use). The provider bears the responsibility of locating a source of randomness. Most providers simply rely on the highest-priority provider that implements the SHA1PRNG algorithm through the SecureRandom engine. If there is a specific CSPRNG algorithm you want used in the generation of the key, the second init() method allows you to simply pass an instance of SecureRandom, using it to generate a default length key. The final algorithm independent init() method is the best of both worlds where you provide the desired key length and the source of randomness.

In all cases, when algorithm-specific initialization parameters are required, it is the provider's responsibility to include (and document) appropriate defaults.

2.3.2 Algorithm Specific Initialization

In situations where you always want a particular cipher algorithm to be used, you may want to specify algorithm-specific initialization parameters. The KeyGenerator engine facilitates this by providing two additional overloaded init() methods that support this approach:

```
init(AlgorithmParameterSpec params)

init(AlgorithmParameterSpec params, SecureRandom random)
```

Each of these init() methods require the use of a javax.crypto.spec.AlgorithmParameter Spec instance. Inspecting the JDK's JavaDocs reveals that AlgorithmParameterSpec is merely a marker interface. By marker interface we mean that the interface defines no formal public methods or static constants, identical in concept to the more commonly used java.io.Serializable interface. This architecture allows the provider to define virtually *any* class as an algorithm parameter by simply including the AlgorithmParameterSpec marker interface. The first init() method is similar to the algorithm independent init(int keySize) method in that the provider bears the responsibility of locating a source of randomness, where the second init() method dictates a specific CSPRNG algorithm.

2.3.3 Obtaining the Symmetric Cipher Key via SecretKey Class

Each cipher may have different requirements for its secret key. For this reason, keys are hidden behind a series of interfaces. The top-level interface is the Key interface, and it defines three easy to understand methods:

- getAlgorithm() returns the String name of the algorithm, e.g. "Blowfish"
- getFormat() returns the String name of the encoding format of the key data
- getEncoded() returns a byte[] representing the key in the above encoding format

The KeyGenerator engine always returns a SecretKey instance, for example:

```
KeyGenerator kg = KeyGenerator.getInstance("Blowfish");

SecretKey key = kg.generateKey();


//Grab the raw bytes of the key and prepare to represent generically

byte[] myKey = desKey.getEncoded();
```

A SecretKey object declares no additional public methods or constants beyond those defined by the Key interface, and is used solely to logically group symmetric keys.

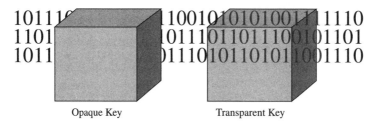

Figure 2.2: Opaque keys hide their details while transparent expose their meta-data.

2.4   Avoiding Opaque Keys

The result of the generateKey() method on the KeyGenerator engine is a provider-specific, opaque key. Our use of opaque here means that the key is treated as a black box where we don't know much beyond the fact that a key was generated, as depicted in Figure 2.2. There is no mechanism at the SecretKey level to find out meta-data about the key (e.g., is the key considered to be weak?).

To facilitate the ability to find out more about the key than just the three pieces of data exposed by the SecretKey class, the JCE offers two mechanisms for translating a secret key into a symmetric cipher *key specification* that is provider-independent, and vice versa.

1. The first approach is through the combination of the SecretKeyFactory class and another class that implements the KeySpec marker interface
2. The second approach is through the javax.crypto.spec.SecretKeySpec class.

Once the secret key has been translated into a key specification, a level of transparency has been achieved. This transparency allows us to "look into" the key and at its meta-data. As we'll see shortly using DES as an example, this transparency can ensure that a strong key has been selected.

2.4.1   Code Example: Converting a Key into a Key Specification, Option 1

The provider may directly use a KeySpec interface, but most often a specific class is usually used that implements the KeySpec interface. Many examples are found in the java.security.spec package. For example, this package defines a DESKeySpec class that describes a DES key in a provider-independent way. It declares several methods used for interrogating meta-data about the key, for example, a method that can determine if the key is considered weak or semiweak and should be thrown away.

By exposing the key's meta-data as a key specification in this manner, it becomes possible to plug into different providers for different parts of the cryptographic operation, that is, a DES key generated from a SecureRandom CSPRNG from the SunJCE provider could then be fed into a Bouncy Castle DES cipher. In some situations, this happens behind the scenes without explicit knowledge. Remember, both the KeyGenerator engine and the soon-to-be discussed Cipher engine operate using the standard pair of engine factory methods. By definition, when no provider is explicitly specified, these factory methods rely on a consistent priority search pattern based on the provider declarations found in the java.security file. Therefore, it is not difficult to envision a situation where the KeyGenerator may come from one provider, and the Cipher from yet another.

Each provider is required to document which key specifications they support, for example the SunJCE provider supplies the aforementioned DESKeySpec as a transparent representation of DES keys. Consider the following code sample that generates a key for use in a DES cipher using the highest priority provider that implements a DES secret key factory:

Example 2.2 Sample Code Location: com.mkp.jce.chap2.KeyToKeySpecConversion

```
1  byte[] myKey = ... //a byte array that is your DES key

2

3  try

4  {

5    DESKeySpec desKeySpec = new DESKeySpec(myKey);

6    try

7    {

8      SecretKeyFactory factory = SecretKeyFactory.getInstance("DES");

9      try

10     {

11       SecretKey key = factory.generateSecret(desKeySpec);

12

13       //The SecretKey instance is now ready to be passed to a cipher

14       //instance as the key for an encryption or decryption operation

15

16     } catch (InvalidKeySpecException ike)

17     {

18       //The key provided doesn't pass the SecretKeyFactor rules!
```

```
19    }

20

21  } catch (NoSuchAlgorithmException nsae)

22  {

23     //There is no provider that can fulfill our request for a DES

24  }

25

26  } catch (InvalidKeyException ike)

27  {

28     //The key provided doesn't pass the key spec rules!

29  }
```

For illustration purposes, imagine the byte array on line 1 is populated from a user-entered pass phrase from your GUI and converted to a byte array through the getBytes() method found on the String class. This would avoid the use of the KeyGenerator altogether, relying entirely on the randomness of human nature. The DESKeySpec class created on line 5 exposes the additional meta-data previously described, presuming the key meets the minimal requirements (e.g., 56 bits of data). For example, DES has 16 known *weak* or *dual keys* [7] where a weak key is defined as a key that has the unfortunate property that double encryption (simply encrypting twice) returns the original plaintext. The following keys are documented in FIPS-74 [8] as weak:

	KEY	DUAL
1.	E001E001F101F101	01E001E001F101F1
2.	FE1FFE1FFE0EFE0E	1FFE1FFE0EFE0EFE
3.	E01FE01FF10EF10E	1FE01FE00EF10EF1
4.	01FE01FE01FE01FE	FE01FE01FE01FE01
5.	011F011F010E010E	1F011F010E010E01
6.	E0FEE0FEF1FEF1FE	FEE0FEE0FEF1FEF1
7.	0101010101010101	0101010101010101
8.	FEFEFEFEFEFEFEFE	FEFEFEFEFEFEFEFE
9.	E0E0E0E0F1F1F1F1	E0E0E0E0F1F1F1F1
10.	1F1F1F1F0E0E0E0E	1F1F1F1F0E0E0E0E

Note that the first 6 keys have duals different than themselves, hence each is a key and a dual giving 12 keys with duals. The last 4 keys equal their duals, rounding out the field of 16 keys to avoid. No other keys are known to exist that have duals.

When the generateSecret() method is invoked on line 18, the provider specific instance of the SecretKeyFactory may scrutinize the meta-data more closely than the DESKeySpec constructor did on line 6. While the SunJCE provider does not appear to perform this check, other providers could query the isWeak() method inside the generateSecret() method on line 18 and throw an InvalidKeySpecException that refuses the key if it is in the list of keys documented in FIPS-74.

Let's continue with the idea that our byte array on line 1 originated from user input. We could perform the weak key check ourselves easily. One if statement is all we would have to code to check the key:

```
if(DesKeySpec.isWeak(myKey,

{

        //Choose a different pass phrase to generate a key from

}
```

Since the set of weak keys is so small, there is a negligible impact on performance to include the weak key check.

To recap, the use of classes that implement the KeySpec interface provide us and providers with transparent key access. This transparency provides the ability for further interrogation of the key and its meta-data to ensure it is adequate for use in the named algorithm.

2.4.2   Code Example: Converting a Key into a Key Specification, Option 2

The SecretKeySpec class can be used as a shortcut to a provider-independent key specification, avoiding the provider based SecretKeyFactory engine altogether. Realistically, this option is only viable for symmetric ciphers that require a sole byte array for their key specification. Ciphers requiring more than a byte array will be forced to use the engine method described in Option 1. Notice how much smaller this code block is compared to the SecretKeyFactory sample in Option 1:

```
byte[] myKey = ...// an array of bytes that represent your DES key


//create a provider independent secret key for a DES cipher

SecretKeySpec key = new SecretKeySpec(myKey, "DES");
```

Close inspection of the SecretKeySpec class reveals that it implements the Key, KeySpec, SecretKey, and Serializable interfaces. That means that the result of this operation can be passed to any method expecting any one of the first three interfaces, and the result could be serialized for later use. Additionally, since the input data is so relatively simple (a byte array), there are no exceptions thrown from the constructor that have to be handled.

However, at the cost of simplicity we forgo the possibility of key and key metadata inspections. For example, the JavaDocs of the SecretKeySpec clearly indicate that this method doesn't even ensure that 8-bytes (56-bits) worth of data are present to create a DES key. It is because of this severe limitation that you should stick to Option 1 above and avoid the SecretKeySpec approach in most situations.

2.5 Categorizing Symmetric Ciphers

One way symmetric ciphers can be categorized is based on how they actually perform their encryption. There are two broad categories of ciphers, block and stream, and they are depicted in Figure 2.3.

A **Block Cipher** operates on a chunk of data (i.e., "a block") at once, typically 64- or 128-bits. Figure 2.3 depicts that until enough plaintext shows up for encryption, the block cipher essentially sits and waits. In contrast, a **Stream Cipher** operates against a single byte at a time. Figure 2.3 depicts that as a byte of data is ready for encryption,

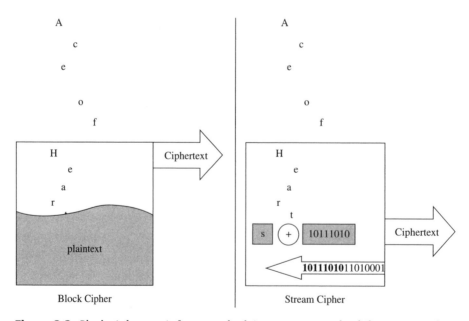

Figure 2.3: Block ciphers wait for enough plaintext to proceed, while stream ciphers work on what is available.

the plaintext is combined with bits from a *Keystream Generator*. Keystream Generators are responsible for producing a sequence of random bits. If the keystream was a pure-random sequence—not pseudo-random, but purely random, we would achieve what is known as a **One Time Pad**—the perfect encryption. The problem lies in generating true random numbers, and then sharing that sequence of random numbers with the intended recipient(s). The mathematical power behind a streaming cipher is the *exclusive or* (XOR) operation, identified by the symbol $\oplus$ in the figure. Mathematically speaking, $N \oplus 0 = N$, so if the keystream is a repeating sequence of zeros, then absolutely no encryption is performed and the result is the original plaintext message. More advanced streaming ciphers ensure that multiple encryptions of identical plaintext messages results in dissimilar ciphertexts.

Generally speaking, block ciphers are most effective when used to encode a single message where the size is known ahead of time. A common characteristic of a block cipher is that multiple encryptions of identical plaintext blocks with an identical secret key result in identical ciphertexts (we'll show how this can be overcome next when we introduce cipher modes). Alternatively, when the flow of plaintext is unknown, for example TCP/IP communications, a streaming cipher is considered a more effective and efficient solution.

Regardless of category, a symmetric cipher has three things that you must always keep in mind when implementing your software. The three things to consider include *key management*, *data integrity*, and *non-repudiation*. Let's discuss each of these issues.

2.5.1 Key Management

Symmetric ciphers work great when you don't have to distribute the secret key. For example, if Alice has some files that you want to protect from prying eyes, a symmetric cipher is an excellent fit. Alice can choose the password, encrypt the files, and Alice simply has to remember the password until she needs to read them again. As long as Alice doesn't tell anyone or write down her password, her files are for all intensive purposes secure. However, let's say that Alice's associate Bob needs access to the files. If Bob lives down the street, Alice could simply drive over to his house and whisper the password in his ear. But what if Bob lived across an ocean? Now Alice is facing a conundrum. How does she communicate to Bob—thousands of miles away, what the password is to access the files, while ensuring that the password isn't intercepted along the way? The next chapter will demonstrate how to leverage the speed and power of a symmetric cipher for encrypting her files, while relying on the strengths of an asymmetric cipher to safely share the symmetric cipher secret key with Bob.

2.5.2 Non-Repudiation

Merriam-Webster defines *repudiate* as "to refuse to have anything to do with." Let's imagine that Alice runs a company that supplies Bob's company with widgets. Alice and Bob decide (poorly) to use a symmetric cipher to exchange purchase orders, invoices, and shipping manifests between each of their companies. They share a common password between them one day over lunch. Alice sends a huge order to Bob's company. Blindly, Bob buys the raw materials and processes them to make the requested number of widgets. He then promptly ships all of the widgets to Alice's company, who then denies ever having placed an order of that magnitude. What recourse does Bob have? Needless to say, this problem raises some serious financial implications for both sides. Non-repudiation is a means of incorporating a form of accountability into the process such that Alice has no basis to make a claim that the order didn't come from her; that order *had* to come from Alice. Using a symmetric cipher, there is no way for Bob to verify digitally and guarantee that the order truly came from Alice's company and not some hacker. Anyone—literally *anyone*—who knows the secret key could encrypt a message and forge a PO from Alice to Bob. This example demonstrates the lack of inherent non-repudiation facilities in a symmetric cipher. Chapter 4 will demonstrate how documents can be digitally signed using an asymmetric cipher, providing a high level of non-repudiation.

2.5.3   Data Integrity

For the most part, symmetric ciphers can avoid most data integrity problems by understanding the structure of the resulting ciphertext. Imagine a ciphertext where there is no tie from the current block to the previous or next block of ciphertext. While this may work well, for example, inside of a database where you may only want to decipher one record of data at a time, it can carry serious consequences in network communications or similar applications. Blocks could easily be added or removed, with no way to verify the overall integrity of the message. The block may be valid, but it may not have been part of the original message. The classic example is a plain text message that reads "Attack At Dawn" which is intercepted by the enemy, who promptly adds a rogue block in front of the message: "Do Not Attack At Dawn." The recipient deciphers the message cleanly and takes no action the next morning.

To understand how to manage these data integrity issues, cipher algorithms are often complemented with a cipher mode. Let's look at the role message padding and cipher modes play in addressing data integrity.

2.6   **Padding and Cipher Modes**

Often we speak of a cipher algorithm, for example an instance of a DES cipher, but the reality is that the cipher engine rarely works with just a cipher algorithm. The reality is that the cipher likely employs a cipher mode and a padding scheme as well. To fully comprehend how to build our cipher engine algorithm request, we have to understand these two concepts as well. Let's take a look at different padding schemes and cipher modes.

2.6.1 Padding

Padding is required when the plaintext length is too short for the cipher to complete successfully; so "padded" bits are added. The JCE supports four distinct padding mechanisms (though providers are free to support as many different padding mechanisms as they wish):

- None

- PKCS5Padding

- SSL3Padding (reserved word, not implemented according to JDK documentation)

- OAEPWith<digest>And<mgf>Padding

As the name implies, with None no padding is applied. It is your responsibility to ensure that the plaintext is of an appropriate length prior to encryption. SSL3Padding padding is only slightly different than the PKCS #5 padding scheme, and the SunJCE provider included with JDK 1.4.1 out of the box doesn't support this padding scheme—but other providers may offer support. Optimal Asymmetric Encryption Padding (OAEP is a padding scheme defined in PKCS #1 by RSA Laboratories) is one of the more complex padding mechanisms. OAEP requires a message digest (e.g., MD5) and something known as a *mask generation function*. For our purposes here, we are going to oversimplify the mask generation function by defining it as a variable length hash. Message digests and hashing is covered in-depth in Chapter 4.

PKCS stands for Public Key Cryptography Standard, and represents many different de facto public key standards as published by RSA Laboratories. PKCS #5 is one of the more common mechanisms used by various symmetric ciphers to pad their messages, and the one we'll be using the most in our code samples. This padding format was originally defined in RFC 1423. This padding mechanism uses the message plaintext to calculate the number of positions shy of an even block multiple. This number of bytes are then appended to the message, using the number as the value. For example, using hexadecimal notation the following are all valid pads, where 01 represents that only 1 byte of padding was necessary and 08 represents that 8 bytes were necessary:

01

0202

030303

04040404

0505050505

060606060606

07070707070707

0808080808080808

Thus, the last byte of the last block is *always* indicative of the number of padding bytes employed by the block, allowing the padding to be stripped off after decryption. *Every* message must be padded under this approach. In the event the message size is an exact multiple of the block size being employed, one complete block of padding must be attached, for example 0808080808080808.

2.6.2   Cipher Modes

A cryptographic **Cipher Mode** represents the combination of a strong cipher algorithm plus a simple feedback or noise operation. The goal of this mode is to "hide" plaintext blocks that might be repeated throughout the message. There are numerous cryptographic modes available; we're going to restrict our scope here to only a few. The Sun JCE supports the following cipher modes, among others:

NONE/ECB

CBC

CFB

Electronic Codebook Mode (ECB)

In this mode, a key is fed into the block cipher, which takes one plaintext block and generates one ciphertext block. If the message happens to contain identical blocks, in each case identical ciphertext blocks are produced. One benefit of ECB is that the message doesn't have to be encrypted linearly, since each block is effectively its own independent message. Consider the example of an encrypted database table. It would be extremely expensive to decrypt the entire table each time a row in the middle of the table was being accessed. Since the definition of a database table is static, it is elementary to calculate the required block size so that each row corresponded to a block. In this way, only the randomly accessed row in the table would have to be decrypted, not the entire table.

ECB is fast, but it is by far the weakest cipher mode because no attempt is made to hide patterns in the plaintext. Usually you'll want to use either CBC or CFB for your cipher mode.

Cipher Block Chaining (CBC)

This mode introduces a feedback mechanism into the encryption process such that each block is dependent on all of the previous blocks before it. CBC employs an XOR operation between the plaintext and the previous ciphertext block, as demonstrated in Figure 2.4. Before the next plaintext block is fed into the cipher engine, the previous ciphertext block is XOR'ed with the incoming plaintext block. The result of this XOR operation is then fed into the cipher engine for encryption using the provided secret key.

Decryption simply reverses the process. This chaining mechanism addresses the major weakness of ECB—identical plaintext blocks result in identical ciphertext blocks.

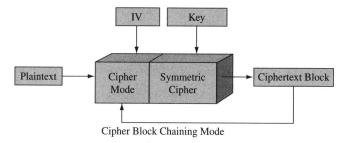

Cipher Block Chaining Mode

Figure 2.4: CBC relies on the previous ciphertext block to provide "noise" that hides plaintext patterns.

CBC overcomes this ECB problem so long as the proceeding ciphertext blocks are different for each identical plaintext block. The first block of plaintext to be encrypted has no "previous" block to draw ciphertext feedback from. As a result, an **Initialization Vector** (IV) is needed to prime the encryption operation. The IV has no meaningful relation to the plaintext. In fact, its sole purpose is to populate the feedback registers inside of the cipher mode box because there was no preceding ciphertext block to do the job. Often a time stamp or simply random bits from the SecureRandom engine are used as the IV. There is nothing confidential about the IV; the strength of the cipher remains with the secret key. Therefore, transmission of the IV in plaintext has no direct impact on the strength of the ciphertext [12].

Cipher FeedBack Mode (CFB)

When employing a CBC mode, encryption simply isn't possible until a full block of data has been received. For example, consider something like TCP/IP network transmissions. The cipher would have to passively wait for enough data before it could encrypt and transmit, creating network latency in the process. Cipher Feedback Mode essentially resolves this problem by effectively transposing a block cipher into a stream cipher. Any block cipher using CFB requires the use of an initialization vector that *must* be different for every message being sent. We can see the IV initializing the cipher mode in Figure 2.5. Where CBC pushes incoming plaintext into a queue, letting the queue grow until an appropriate block size is reached, CFB immediately takes that plaintext byte and applies an XOR with first byte from the front of the keystream.

The effect of pushing these bits back onto the keystream makes each byte of ciphertext dependent on the preceding plaintext, similar to CBC, but with the advantage of operating as a stream cipher.

At this point we've covered the formal definition of a symmetric cipher and the importance of the key. We've also looked at several cipher modes and described various

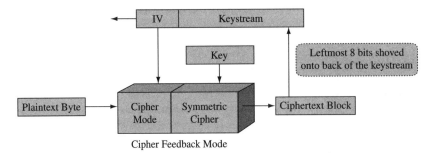

Cipher Feedback Mode

Figure 2.5: CFB dynamically builds a "keystream" by placing the leftmost byte of the ciphertext block onto the back of the keystream. Before a byte of plaintext is pushed into the cipher engine it is XOR'ed with the a byte from the front of the keystream.

padding mechanisms that create ideal block sizes. With all of this information, we are finally ready to focus on the JCE's Cipher engine and how we can use Java to turn plaintext into ciphertext.

2.7 The Cipher Engine

The Cipher class serves as the entry point into all of the JCE cipher algorithms. Its nomenclature is consistent with every other JCA engine discussed in the preceding chapter, relying on the use of the standard pair of engine factory methods.

> Note: A small discrepancy in terminology exists between the JCA documentation and the JCE documentation. The JCA documentation refers to an "algorithm" argument in its factory methods, while the JCE describes the same argument as a "transformation" argument. Throughout this book, we will use the JCA terminology when discussing an engine's factory methods.

Thus far, we have described the Cipher engine's factory method as accepting an "algorithm" parameter. We need to slightly elaborate on this definition. The following code example is perfectly valid syntax:

```
Cipher desCipher = Cipher.getInstance("DES");
```

While this statement will return an instance of a DES cipher, the reality is that the cipher is more than just a "DES" cipher—it most likely employs a mode and a padding scheme as well. But which cipher mode and padding scheme are being employed when only the cipher algorithm is specified? The answer is, *it depends*. According to the JCE specification, when no explicitly specified cipher mode and padding scheme are specified, the choice is left to the provider. So what provider did the cipher engine use? The answer once again is, *it depends!* Remember, the architecture of the JCE gives you as much or as little control as you want. The ability to request a "DES" cipher algorithm is certainly valid, but you in effect give up your right to choose a provider, a cipher mode, and a padding scheme.

Any *user* can modify their java.security **file whenever they get the urge; never make any assumptions that a certain provider will always be first in the list!**

In the previous code example, without doing a lot of detective work, we don't know which provider was used, what cipher mode was employed, or what padding scheme has been applied. The SunJCE provider explicitly documents that the DES, DES-EDE and Blowfish ciphers each use ECB as the default cipher mode and PKCS5Padding as the default padding scheme. For comparison, imagine another provider *AnotherProvider* that also supports the DES cipher. Their default cipher mode is CBC. What happens if these two providers were paired together, one for encryption and the other for decryption? Using machine *a* with a nonmodified java.security file, the SunJCE would theoretically be the first provider found that offers a DES solution. You encrypt some plaintext and write it out to a floppy disk. Later, you use machine *b* to attempt to decrypt the same ciphertext. The key specification was serialized, and as demonstrated earlier in this chapter, is provider independent and thus equally usable on both machines despite their different configurations. Unfortunately, the decryption is all garbled. How can that be? Well, machine *b* used a modified java.security file that listed the *AnotherProvider* provider ahead of all others that offered DES. Since the cipher modes differed (the SunJCE used ECB by default, *AnotherProvider* used CBC), the output is worthless.

In any situation where the full-cycle cryptographic process (encryption and decryption) spans multiple JVMs (realize each JVM could theoretically be configured differently, even if they are on the same machine!), listing only the name of the desired cipher is like playing a game of Russian roulette and is ill-advised.

Overcoming the cipher mode and padding scheme ambiguity problem is easy. The algorithm argument of each Cipher factory method supports the explicit naming of the cipher mode and padding scheme. The following format is available beyond listing only the name of the algorithm, and it is highly suggested that this format is always used to avoid the situation just described.

```
algorithm/mode/padding e.g. DES/CBC/PKCS5Padding
```

Passing DES/CBC/PKCS5Padding to the Cipher factory method informs the engine that you want a provider that can offer you a DES encryption algorithm that employs Cipher Block Chaining as a feedback mode and applies a PKCS#5 padding scheme to the plaintext.

Each provider will typically document the formal and aliased names assigned to their algorithms. I tend to keep the CompletEngineListing sample from Chapter 1 in my CLASSPATH. Anytime I need to lookup an alias, I just fire it off and immediately I see my available choices. In fact, you may consider integrating this class as an external tool into your IDE!

Form the habit of being as specific as possible with any JCE engine, Cipher engine or otherwise, when requesting a specific algorithm. Let's revisit our example from moments ago, this time explicitly requesting a cipher mode and padding scheme:

```
Cipher desCipher = Cipher.getInstance("DES/ECB/PKCS5Padding");
```

When this line of code executes on machine *a* with the SunJCE provider, encryption is performed identical to the previous example since we declared the same defaults the SunJCE provider used. Machine *b* will now successfully decrypt our information, since the *AnotherProvider* provider now knows what specific cipher mode and padding scheme to use.

The previous example leads to an important concept when dealing with any cryptographic topic: *ambiguity is dangerous*, regardless of where the ambiguity lies, be it in the cipher or the cipher mode or the padding scheme. Cryptography is based on the strong shoulder of mathematic principles. There is no reason to broadcast such information, but even if someone intercepted your ciphertext and knew that it was encrypted using the Blowfish algorithm with a CBC feedback mode and a PKCS #5 padding scheme, the data are still essentially safe provided you used a sound secret key. If you ever run across some provider that refuses to let their cipher implementation be scrutinized by cryptanalysts and mathematicians, be very leery of trusting sensitive data to that algorithm.

2.7.1   Initializing the Engine

After obtaining an instance of a Cipher object that implements the cipher, cipher mode, and padding scheme specified, an additional initialization step must occur. Why is this step necessary? Well, it's as simple as informing the engine about which mode of operation you are interested in, that is, encryption or decryption. At any given moment in time, the cipher instance can only encrypt or decrypt, not both. Beyond that, the initialization is also where we provide the engine with the secret key that it should use. This initialization is through one of the engine's overloaded init() methods.

There are several important characteristics of the init() method that you should be aware of. Perhaps the most important side effect of invoking any init() method is that the cipher engine's state is completely reset; it's like having a newly constructed cipher at that point. If you had several discrete pieces of data that you wanted to encrypt with different keys, invoke the Cipher engine's factory method to obtain your cipher instance, then invoke the init() method three times, passing a different secret key each time. Another consideration is that if the init() method invoked doesn't provide enough information to adequately initialize a cipher set to operate in an encryption mode, then the cipher implementation is expected to generate the remaining parameters. A strong example of this is providing only a secret key to the init() method, yet the cipher mode requires the presence of an initialization vector (IV). The opposite case however is not true. If the cipher was placed into decryption mode, and no IV is provided, decryption cannot continue because a randomly generated IV cannot successfully decrypt the data. In this case, an exception would be thrown from the init() method eluding to the problem.

2.7.2 Code Example: Block Cipher Encryption

In the interest of brevity, we aren't going to cover each of the eight overloaded init() methods found on the Cipher engine. Instead, we are going to cover the predominate method sufficient for most symmetric algorithms. The method has the following signature:

```
public void init(int opmode, Key key);
```

The opmode argument is a directive to the cipher that indicates if it should initialize itself for encryption or decryption. For a symmetric cipher, use the static constants Cipher.ENCRYPT_MODE or Cipher.DECRYPT_MODE instead of a literal int value. The key argument represents the the SecretKey we obtained earlier. The cipher will use this key to perform the specified operation. Depending on the cipher mode employed, the Cipher engine may need to dynamically generate an IV as well (available later for retrieval through the getIV() method). Let's look at a more complete code example:

Example 2.3 Sample Code Location: com.mkp.jce.chap2.BlockCipherEncryption Example

```
1   //Get an instance of a KeyGenerator engine for DES encryption
2   try
3   {
4       KeyGenerator kg = KeyGenerator.getInstance("DES");
5
6       //Here we could optionally pass a key size and a CSPRNG source
7       //In this code example, we'll use whatever defaults the provider uses
8
9       SecretKey key = kg.generateKey();
10
11      //Translate our key into its encoded byte array
12      byte[] desKey = key.getEncoded();
13
14      //Use Option 2 to turn the key into a key specification
15      //This approach does not require a try…catch block
16      SecretKeySpec keySpec = new SecretKeySpec(desKey, "DES");
17
18      try
```

```
19  {
20     //Find a provider for a DES cipher algorithm
21     //The provider must use ECB as the cipher mode
22     //and apply a PKCS #5 padding scheme
23     Cipher cipher = Cipher.getInstance("DES/ECB/PKCS5Padding");
24
25     //Initialize the cipher for encryption
26     //and give it the key it should use
27     cipher.init(Cipher.ENCRYPT_MODE, keySpec);
28  } catch (NoSuchAlgorithmException nsae)
29  {
30     //DES cipher using ECB cipher mode with PKCS #5 padding isn't available
31  } catch (InvalidKeyException ike)
32  {
33     //Highly unlikely that SecretKey from KeyGenerator engine would get here
34  } catch (NoSuchPaddingException nspe)
35  {
36     //Padding requested couldn't be found
37  }
38 } catch (NoSuchAlgorithmException nsae)
39 {
40   //DES isn't available; must not have SunJCE in your java.security list
41 }
```

In this code listing, we have a fully initialized cipher, one that is ready to perform an encryption operation. This sample uses a KeyGenerator in lines 4 and 9 to generate a DES key for our encryption operation. Since no init() method calls were made on the Key-Generator instance on line 6, we have deferred the key size and the source of randomness for the key to the provider being used, in this case an opaque algorithm strategy was employed so we don't really have any indication without doing some detective work to find out what provider is fulfilling our request. Once we have our key, lines 12 through 16 convert it to a provider-independent key specification. On line 23, we use an opaque algorithm strategy to obtain a DES cipher using an ECB cipher mode and a PKCS #5 padding scheme. If this is an unmodified Sun JVM, then the java.security file will indicate that the SunJCE provider has the highest priority, and it can fulfill this request. We initialize our cipher on line 27, telling it we are going to perform an encryption operation using the provider-independent key specification previously obtained on line 16. At this point, we are ready to perform encryption using this cipher.

Once the cipher is properly initialized, there is nothing standing in the way of performing an actual encryption operation. The Cipher object defines a robust interface for accomplishing encryption, allowing you to determine the most efficient and suitable approach for the plaintext data and its source. Two sets of overloaded methods are defined, including four different update() methods and six different doFinal() methods. The encryption process can work as a single-part or multipart operation, using either one of these two recipes:

Recipe #1: Single-part operation where a small or manageable byte array (perhaps obtained from myString.getBytes() method) only requires a single invocation of the doFinal() method:

```
27    cipher.init(Cipher.ENCRYPT_MODE, keySpec);


      byte[] cipherText =
            cipher.doFinal("this war starts after sunrise".getBytes("UTF-8"));


      //Send your encrypted data to a target here, e.g. to a file


28  } catch (NoSuchAlgorithmException nsae) ...
```

Recipe #2: Multipart operation where a large amount of data, possibly coming from disparate sources (file 1, file 2, and file 3), issues a series of update() method calls, followed by one and only one call to a doFinal() method:

```
27    cipher.init(Cipher.ENCRYPT_MODE, keySpec);


      cipher.update(myByteArray);
      cipher.update(anotherByteArray);
      byte[] cipherText = cipher.doFinal();


      //Send your encrypted data to a target here, e.g. to a file
28  } catch (NoSuchAlgorithmException nsae) ...
```

While there are many combinations of update() and doFinal(), most block cipher applications tend to only need to use Recipe #1, making a single call to doFinal(). Calling either doFinal() or update() means you have to be prepared to catch two additional exceptions, BadPaddingException and IllegalBlockSizeException.

2.7.3   Code Example: Secure Streaming Cipher Encryption

It is worth re-enforcing a concept on the difference between a block cipher and a streaming cipher. Arguably, one could make the statement that a streaming cipher is just a block cipher that operates on a block site that equates to a single byte, for example. 8-bits at a time. It is a trivial operation to turn any block cipher into a streaming cipher with the JCE. When building the *algorithm/cipher mode/padding scheme* string that is fed to one of the standard engine factory methods, the cipher mode supports an additional subformat of <mode><bit count> to specify how many bits to process at a time.

Once we configure the number of bits that the cipher should process at a time, we can then easily wrap any Java InputStream with either the CipherInputStream or CipherOutputStream. Each of these cipher streams take their cue from the Cipher used to initialize them. In order words, if the Cipher is initialized for encryption, then any data passing through the stream is encrypted. Likewise, if the Cipher is initialized for decryption, then any data passing through the stream is decrypted.

The following code sample reads a text file named *plaintext.txt* from the root directory and prints out the corresponding ciphertext to a file named *ciphertext.txt*.

Example 2.4 Sample Code Location: com.mkp.jce.chap2.StreamingCipherEncryption Example

---

```
//Get an instance of a KeyGenerator engine for DES encryption
try
{
        KeyGenerator kg = KeyGenerator.getInstance("DES");


        //Here we could optionally pass a key size and a CSPRNG source
        //In this code example, we'll use whatever defaults the provider uses


        SecretKey key = kg.generateKey();


        //Translate our key into its encoded byte array
        byte[] desKey = key.getEncoded();
```

```
//Use Option 2 to turn the key into a key specification
//This approach does not require a try…catch block
SecretKeySpec keySpec = new SecretKeySpec(desKey, "DES");

try
{
            //Find a provider for a DES cipher algorithm
            //The provider must use CFB as the cipher mode,
            //processing 8 bits at a time through the stream
            //and apply a PKCS #5 padding scheme
            Cipher cipher =
                         Cipher.getInstance("DES/CFB8/PKCS5Padding");

            //Initialize the cipher for encryption
            //and give it the key it should use
            cipher.init(Cipher.ENCRYPT_MODE, keySpec);


                  try
                        {
                        CipherInputStream cis = new CipherInputStream(
                                    new FileInputStream(
                                          new File("/plaintext.txt")), cipher);

                        FileOutputStream fos = new FileOutputStream(
                                  new File("/ciphertext.txt"));

                        //Let's read 64-bits of data per pass. We call this
                        //cipherText since we never actually see the plaintext-
                        //it will be encrypted by the time we see it!
```

```
                byte[] cipherTextBytes = new byte[8];
                int i=0;

                while((i=cis.read(cipherTextBytes)) != -1)
                {
                        fos.write(cipherTextBytes, 0, i);
                }
                System.out.println("All Done!");
            } catch (IOException ioe)
                {
                //Handle this!
                }
```

```
} catch (NoSuchAlgorithmException nsae)
{
//A DES cipher using an CFB cipher mode of 8-bits processing
//with PKCS #5 padding isn't available
        //Handle this!
} catch (InvalidKeyException ike)
{
        //Highly unlikely that a SecretKey from
        //a KeyGenerator engine would get here
        //However, we never assume!
        //Handle this!
} catch (NoSuchPaddingException nspe)
{
//Handle this!
}
}
} catch (NoSuchAlgorithmException nsae)
{
        //DES isn't available;
```

```
    //must not have SunJCE in your java.security list!

    //Handle this!

}
```

The algorithm is remarkably similar to the BlockCipherEncryptionExample class we looked at earlier in this chapter. There are two sections where the code differs from that example, and we'll narrow our focus to them. The first section is the factory method invocation. We've modified our request to use a streaming feedback mode (CFB, in this example) that processes 8-bits of data per cycle. Since we have switched to a CFB feedback mode, the cipher requires an IV to prime the operation. Since we don't explicitly provide one, the Cipher engine will dynamically generate one. We have to access the generated IV via the getIV() method of the cipher instance—without it we won't be able to decrypt the ciphertext. The next section uses standard Java InputStream piping, where we open up a File using a FileInputStream and pipe its data through our CipherInputStream. We can see that the CipherInputStream's constructor was provided an initialized Cipher instance. As we process the stream using traditional Java I/O techniques, we never actually have access to the plaintext, immediately receiving the ciphertext from the CipherInputStream.

Example 2.5 Sample Code Location: com.mkp.jce.chap2.StreamingCipherEncryption SaveKey

The StreamingCipherEncryptionSaveKey class is identical to the example we just covered, the StreamingCipherEncryptionExample class, except it prints out and saves the cipher key and the initialization vector so they can be used in our forthcoming decryption example. To conserve space, it is not printed here because it is identical except for the added Java I/O calls.

> Note: We save out the secret key to a plain file here because we don't introduce the notion of a key store until Chapter 5. We are saving it out to a file here for educational purposes; normally, you wouldn't want to save out your secret key like this—in plain sight, and typically you would use a key store. If you are in a hurry to see how to use a key store to hold a symmetric key, you can flip ahead to sections 5.3.2 and 5.3.3 for examples.

2.7.4   Code Example: Secure Streaming Cipher Decryption

If you haven't done so already, you'll need to run the StreamingCipherEncryptionSaveKey code sample. This sample reads a text file named *plaintext.txt* from the root directory and prints out the corresponding ciphertext to a file named *ciphertext.txt*, also in the root directory. In addition to the ciphertext, it writes out the DES key and the IV used in the encryption operation—both pieces of data needed to decrypt the ciphertext.

The decryption process differs only slightly from the encryption process. Previously, we relied on the cipher instance to dynamically generate an IV because one was not explicitly provided. For decryption, this is not an option, and failure to present the exact same IV that was used in the encryption operation means we cannot successfully decrypt the ciphertext. Let's see how we accomplish this:

Example 2.6 Sample Code Location: com.mkp.jce.chap2.StreamingCipherDecryption Example

```
1   try
2   {
3       //Read in the key from the file
4       //NOTE:      Chapter 5 introduces you to the KeyStore, the
5       //           correct way to store a symmetric key!
6       FileInputStream fisKey = new FileInputStream(new File("/mykey.txt"));
7       byte[] desKey = new byte[fisKey.available()];
8       fisKey.read(desKey);
9       fisKey.close();
10
11      //Read in the IV from the file
12      //There is nothing secret about an IV; it can be saved like this
13      FileInputStream fisIV = new FileInputStream(new File("/myIV.txt"));
14      byte[] IV = new byte[fisIV.available()];
15      fisIV.read(IV);
16      fisIV.close();
17
18      try
19      {
20              //Turn our raw bytes into a SecretKeySpec
21              SecretKeySpec keySpec = new SecretKeySpec(desKey, "DES");
22
```

```
23          //Turn our IV into an ArgumentParameterSpec
24          IvParameterSpec iv = new IvParameterSpec(IV);
25
26           Cipher cipher = Cipher.getInstance("DES/CFB8/PKCS5Padding");
27
28          //Initialize our cipher with our key, IV
29          cipher.init(Cipher.DECRYPT_MODE, key, iv);
30
31          try
32          {
33                  CipherInputStream cis = new CipherInputStream(
34                          new FileInputStream(
35                              new File("/ciphertext.txt")), cipher);
36
37                  FileOutputStream fos = new FileOutputStream(
38                          new File("/decrypted_ciphertext.txt"));
39
40                  byte[] plainTextBytes = new byte[8];
41                  int i=0;
42
43                  while( (i = cis.read(plainTextBytes )) !=-1)
44                  {
45                          fos.write(plainTextBytes,0, i);
46                  }
47                  fos.close();
48
49          } catch (IOException cipherIoe)
50          {
51                  //Handle this!
52          }
```

```
53      } catch (NoSuchAlgorithmException nsae)
54      {
55             //Handle this
56      } catch (NoSuchPaddingException nspe)
57      {
58             //Handle this
59      } catch (InvalidKeyException ike)
60      {
61             //Handle this
62      } catch (InvalidAlgorithmParameterException e)
63      {
64             //Handle this
65      }
66  } catch (IOException keyIoe)
67  {
68      //Can't read in the key?
69  }
```

First, we read in the raw bytes that represent our 56-bit DES key and the IV used during the encryption process between lines 6 and 16. Using the raw key bytes, we perform a conversion to a SecretKeySpec class on line 21. This is a great example of where the SecretKeySpec option is particularly useful—since the key was already used in an encryption process, we don't really care if the key was weak or not, thus there is no real value in using the SecretKeyFactory approach. We also need to create an instance of an AlgorithmParameterSpec that represents the initialization vector. Recall that this is simply a marker interface with no methods or constants. Specifically, on line 24 we turn our raw IV byte array into an IvParameterSpec. We then provide our secret key and our IV to the cipher's init() method, toggling the cipher's operation mode to Cipher.DECRYPT_MODE on line 29. Once the secret key and IV have been provided to the cipher, we are ready to actually perform our decryption. This example demonstrates using the CipherInputStream to perform a decrypt operation between lines 33 and 47. This is opposite of the previous example, which used the CipherInputStream to perform an encrypt operation, and it demonstrates the flexibility of this design by simply attaching to existing Java

I/O metaphors. If we inspect the resulting decrypted_ciphertext.txt file, we see our original plaintext message.

This example depicts a fully extended exception handling implementation to clearly list each of the exceptions that could arise. It allows the application to respond appropriately to each situation. For example, perhaps the machine attempting the decryption doesn't offer a DES cipher, in which case a NoSuchAlgorithmException would be thrown, or if PKCS #5 padding scheme isn't offered, a NoSuchPaddingException could occur. Or, possibly the secret key has been corrupted, and the cipher engine throws an InvalidKey Exception. Many Java programmers defeat the powerful Java exception handling techniques by throwing (no pun intended) all of these exceptions together into a generic catch (Exception e) catch block. Then, at best, you provide some generic *Umm, something bad happened* message to the end user. When that user calls the help desk, the tech on the line has limited problem solving ideas because they don't know what actually happened. By expanding the exceptions out like we have them here, we can provide a detailed message. If the tech knew that the actual fault was an unsupported padding exception, they could ask the user to send them their java.security file for review.

2.8 Password Based Encryption

Generally speaking, it is advisable to avoid the use of a human-generated pass phrase where possible, instead relying on the randomness of the KeyGenerator/SecureRandom combination. The fact remains that humans tend to choose small, easy to remember words and phrases. If your application requirements justify the use of password based encryption (PBE), then avoid storing the password inside of a java.lang.String object in your code. Why? The Java language specification clearly indicates that String objects are immutable. So while it *appears* that you are assigning new values into one variable declaration, behind the scenes the compiler and the JVM work together to actually create new String instances with the new value, marking the old String eligible for future garbage collection. This simply means that String instances can't be reset after you're done using the password. For this reason, you should always use char arrays when working with passwords. After the password is no longer needed, simply set each char in the array to null, ensuring that the password is forever wiped from memory.

Humans are predictable, and we suffer from limited memory capabilities. In fact, as creatures of habit, we often choose words and phrases that are easy to remember. Many applications store the user's password in plaintext inside of a database table—a security hole waiting to be exposed. Even the database has to store its data on the hard drive ultimately, and nothing stops a hacker from going track to track on the drive to look for information, by-passing the database's authentication routines. Often architects will forgo the storage of the password itself, and instead store a one-way hash of the password in its place. When the user provides their pass phrase, an identical one-way hash algorithm is employed, and the two hash values are compared. If they are equal, then clearly the same password was provided.

There is one serious flaw with this one-way hash design methodology as described. There are an abundance of on-line dictionaries, and the effort required to iterate over a complete dictionary and produce one-way hash results for each word is minimal. If an attacker ever obtained the list of "one-way encrypted" passwords from a company, all they would have to do is compare the hash values from the database with their own list. When they find a match in a matter of seconds, they've also just breached the system's security. This is often referred to as a *dictionary attack* because the use of a dictionary is employed.

Combating the basic dictionary attack involves a little salt. Salt is not an acronym; it is a random string concatenated with passwords [11] to help counter a dictionary attack. The combination of the original password and the random string essentially makes it more difficult to precompute a list of one-way hash values because it grows the key space substantially. Instead of having a list of one-way hash values for each common password, the attacker would now need a list of one-way hash values for each common password-random string combination. It's worth emphasizing that the addition of salt is merely a deterrent and not an impenetrable solution, and in no way does the addition of salt overcome the problems cited about humans choosing their own passwords.

2.8.1   Code Example: Password Based Encryption with a Message Digest and an Encryption Algorithm

In section 2.4.1 we reviewed the KeyToKeySpecConversion code sample that demonstrated and discussed the benefits of using a *key specification* over a key. In particular, the code example used the DESKeySpec class in conjunction with the SecretKeyFactory. The aforementioned problems with String immutability factored into the design of the key specification used when developing password based encryption solutions. In fact, all password related functions defined on the javax.crypto.spec.PBEKeySpec class leverage char[]'s and not String objects.

Password based encryption relies on salt and an *iteration count* to help obfuscate any dictionary-defined words. The iteration count complicates the key derivation function to further protect the password; a minimum of 1000 iterations is recommended [13]. We can provide these two pieces of information and access them later via the PBEKeySpec class because it is a key specification and thus transparent by definition. Neither of these two pieces of information are considered sensitive, and both can be shared in the clear between the sender and the receiver without compromising the strength of the cipher. The following code snippet demonstrates the declaration of 8 bytes of salt, an iteration count, the solicitation of a password, and the construction of a PBEKeySpec class to hold it all:

Example 2.7 Sample Code Location: com.mkp.jce.chap2.PBEExample

```
1  byte[] salt = new byte[] { (byte) 0x3a, (byte)0x44, (byte)0x7f, (byte)0xf1,
2                             (byte)0xa2, (byte)0xe5, (byte)0x87, (byte)0x31 };
```

```
3
4   int iterations = 1000;
5
6   char[] buf = new char[20]; //maximum 20 character password in this example
7   int bufPos = 0;
8
9   try
10  {
11      //Prompt the user for a short password
12      System.out.print("Enter a password> ");
13
14      //Read in a character at a time, shoving it into our buffer
15      while( (buf[bufPos++] = (char) System.in.read()) != '\n') {}
16
17      //Conver the buffer into a password char array
18      //chop off the trailing \n character
19      char[] password = new char[-bufPos];
20      System.arraycopy(buf, 0, password, 0, bufPos);
21
22      //Create a PBE Key Specification,
23      //provide the password, salt, and iteration count
24      PBEKeySpec pbeKeySpec = new PBEKeySpec(password, salt, iterations);
25
26      //Locate a PBE secret key factory
27      SecretKeyFactory factory =
28              SecretKeyFactory.getInstance("PBEWithMD5AndDES");
29
30      //Generate the secret key from the PBEKeySpec
31      SecretKey key = factory.generateSecret(pbeKeySpec);
32
```

```
33      //Locat a PBE cipher
34      Cipher cipher = Cipher.getInstance("PBEWithMD5AndDES");
35
36      //Initialize the cipher for encryption
37      //and give it the key it should use
38      cipher.init(Cipher.ENCRYPT_MODE, key);
39
40      //Encrypt our command line sentence
41      byte[] cipherText = cipher.doFinal(args[0].getBytes());
42
43      //Send your encrypted data to a target here, e.g. to a file
44
45      //Clear out all password references from memory
46      for(int i=0;i<password.length;i++) buf[i] = password[i] = 0;
47
48 } catch (IOException ioe)
49 {
50      //Handle This!
51 } catch (NoSuchAlgorithmException e)
52 {
53      //Handle This!
54 } catch (InvalidKeySpecException e)
55 {
56      //Handle This!
57 } catch (NoSuchPaddingException e)
58 {
59      //Handle This!
60 } catch (InvalidKeyException e)
61 {
62      //Handle This!
```

```
63  } catch (IllegalStateException e)
64  {
65      //Handle This!
66  } catch (IllegalBlockSizeException e)
67  {
68      //Handle This!
69  } catch (BadPaddingException e)
70  {
71      //Handle This!
72  }
```

In this example, we demonstrate the construction of a password key specification on line 24, passing the user-provided password, the random salt bytes, and an iteration count. Different PBE implementations may pull their key bits from different locations. For example, PKCS #5 accesses only 8-bits (low order), while PKCS #12 inspects all 16-bits of each character. To determine which bits a cipher algorithm uses, review the provider's documentation. Lines 27 through 31 show another example of the SecretKeyFactory being used to generate a SecretKey. Once we have the secret key, the cipher request, its initialization, and the ensuing encryption process are identical to previous sample algorithms earlier in this chapter.

By this point you should begin to identify common JCA/JCE coding patterns in our samples. While this is the last Cipher example in this chapter, we will see more examples throughout the rest of this book using this same structure:

1. Obtain the secret key bytes via CSPRNG (preferred) or optionally from a user-provided password obtained via char[]

2. Turn the key into a key specification via a SecretKeyFactory instance (preferred) or alternatively the SecretKeySpec

3. Request an instance of your preferred cipher algorithm via a Cipher instance

4. Initialize your cipher appropriately

5. Encrypt or decrypt your plaintext

6. (store or process your ciphertext/plaintext)

7. Clear any pertinent variables for security. Since CSPRNG passwords appear random, they look like memory noise and resetting them is less of a concern than a user-provided password.

2.9 Bringing Order to Chaos: Picking a Cipher

Despite the newfound knowledge this chapter gave you for working with the JCE's symmetric ciphers, it can still be a daunting task to choose *which* block cipher algorithm to use. The choice can become even more difficult if you factor in providers beyond the standard SunJCE and the algorithms it offers. Each application has its own unique circumstances that prevent me from making an all-encompassing statement like *always use this cipher*. However, this section is intended to give you a bit of nonmathematical insight into the algorithms the SunJCE provider ships with. If pressed into making a public recommendation, my choice would be to rely on the AES cipher.

2.9.1 DES

DES is the grand-daddy of ciphers, and the odds are it is the only cipher name here that makes you scratch your head and go "I've heard of this one before!" Unfortunately, the usefulness of DES is rapidly diminishing. Today's workstations can crack a DES encryption with little-to-no effort. This is, in part, due to the small key (56-bit) and block size (64-bit) of DES. If you're reading this book while designing your software, I suggest you avoid DES entirely and opt for either an AES or Blowfish algorithm.

2.9.2 DESede a.k.a. TripleDES

This cipher isn't a "revolution" at all, and in fact DESede stands for DES-encrypt-decrypt-encrypt. The concept behind this approach was to rectify the small key size of DES. The DES key size was limited to 56-bits. By encrypting the plaintext, then intentionally decrypting it with the wrong key, then encrypt those scrambled results to yield the final ciphertext, the key size was increased to 56-bits * 3, or 168-bits. Simple fractions tell us that DESede is 1/3 of the speed of a DES encryption, and DES isn't considered a thoroughbred racehorse by anyone's standard. Despite the gain in key size, the block size is still very small. This is another algorithm that should be avoided entirely if you are designing your solution today.

2.9.3 Advanced Encryption Standard (AES)

AES is the result of a cryptographic competition backed by NIST. Of the 15 submitted proposals, ultimately the "Rijndael" cipher was selected (which got its name from portions of its two designers' names) as the model for AES. AES uses a 256-bit key, which immediately gives it superior protection characteristics over its distant (read legacy) DES and DESede ancestors. There are many cryptographers who know far more about mathematics than I do, and most of them unequivocally believe that no one will lose their job if they choose to use AES for the encryption needs. If for that reason alone, AES should be in your list of finalists when picking an algorithm.

2.9.4 Blowfish

This nonpatented, public domain cipher was designed by Bruce Schneier, a well-respected cryptologist. Blowfish was designed from scratch to be a fast 64-bit block cipher tuned for today's de facto standard 32-bit architectures. Its key length can be as large as 448-bits. The cost for these benefits comes in the form of memory consumption—frankly, it's a self-admitted memory hog [8]. However, the Bouncy Castle provider includes Blowfish and other algorithms implemented using light-weight API's that run fine on a J2ME/MIDP 1.0 specification phone [9].

## chapter 3

Working with Asymmetric Ciphers and Key Agreement Protocols

Asymmetric ciphers are often used in distributed architectures. Public-Key Cryptography is a common term used to describe asymmetric ciphers; the terms are interchangeable. Key agreement protocols explicitly rely on the design characteristics of asymmetric ciphers. In each situation, two keys are required to successfully employ a round trip cryptographic operation. The two keys are appropriately named **public key** and **private key**, and often they are collectively referred to as a key pair. The two predominate uses of these key pairs include generating digital signatures and performing encryption operations, and they can also be used in agreeing on a common secret key in a key agreement protocol. Not all algorithms support all operations. For example, a DSA key pair can only be used in a digital signature and isn't suitable for encryption operations.

If you've ever received an email that was digitally signed, then you've seen asymmetric ciphers in action. Architecturally speaking, the JCE recycles concepts and engines, and much of the asymmetric work is done from the same Cipher engine introduced in Chapter 2 when we discussed symmetric ciphers. If you've decided to jump straight to this chapter, skipping the last, I encourage you to reevaluate that decision and start by at least skimming through the preceding chapter.

The keys are the critical pieces in an asymmetric cipher. The public key is intended for wide distribution, while the private key must be protected; if the private key is compromised, then so is every message digitally signed and/or encrypted using that key pair. Generally, the private key is used to produce a digital signature, and the public key is used to validate the signature. More specifically, the sender uses the private key, and the receiver uses the public key. It is important to understand that asymmetric ciphers were designed to be two-key systems; the possession of one key doesn't provide enough information to calculate the other, and by itself a single key can't perform a roundtrip sign/verify or encrypt/decrypt operation. Some asymmetric ciphers use key pairs that work both ways, that is, the private key encrypts while the public key decrypts, or the public key encrypts and the private key decrypts. It is imperative that you review the specific capabilities of the asymmetric ciphers you are going to use in your applications.

Chapter 2 discussed three things to keep in mind when incorporating a symmetric cipher into your software designs. These things were *key management*, *data integrity*, and *non-repudiation*. Asymmetric ciphers have two keys, and so naturally key management is doubly important. The issue of non-repudiation is directly addressed by asymmetric ciphers. If a digital signature is decrypted and verified using someone's public key, then mathematically speaking the public key's matching private key *had* to produce that signature. Notice the phrasing there: the private key had to produce the signature, not the person or entity. Anyone who doesn't protect his or her private key still faces a significant risk of impersonation. As for data integrity, asymmetric ciphers that are capable of encryption can also rely on cipher modes to disguise textual patterns and use a padding scheme to supplement incomplete blocks.

Let's revisit Alice's situation originally presented in Chapter 2, section 2.5.1. She needs to send some sensitive files to her associate Bob who lives across the ocean. Alice and Bob decide to leverage public-key cryptography in their quest to protect the data in the files. Bob sends Alice his public key via an e-mail. Alice generates a secret key for use in her symmetric cipher algorithm and encrypts the large files using the fast symmetric algorithm. Alice then uses Bob's public key to encrypt the secret key and forwards the encrypted files and the encrypted key in an e-mail to Bob telling him what symmetric cipher algorithm she used on the files. The *only* key that can be used to decrypt the secret symmetric cipher key is Bob's private key. So long as Bob never shares or loses his private key, only Bob will be able to decrypt the key and in turn decrypt and read the copy of Alice's files. To further clarify, let's say that Eve is a corporate spy. She intercepts Bob's e-mail to Eve—the one that contains Bob's public key. She then successfully intercepts Alice's e-mail back to Bob with the symmetrically encrypted files and the asymmetrically encrypted key. No data will be compromised because only Bob's private key can be used to decrypt the public key's ciphertext, and without the secret key stored in that ciphertext, the data in the files remain protected.

Asymmetric ciphers depend heavily on extremely large prime numbers that have been randomly generated. By extremely large, we mean prime numbers that might have 300 or more digits! Attackers wanting to break an asymmetric cipher typically don't use a brute force attack, opting instead to try and guess the random prime numbers used by the keys. Architecturally speaking, this difference in design makes it nearly impossible to compare the strength and security of a symmetric cipher key to that of an asymmetric cipher key—they are literally apples and oranges. It is worth reiterating that symmetric ciphers are fast and they can encrypt very large chunks of data. Not every asymmetric cipher is suitable for encryption, and many of the algorithms that can perform encryption operations do it slower than a symmetric cipher and are limited in the amount of data they can successfully encrypt. Never discount the ability to combine symmetric and asymmetric ciphers in your solutions.

The first step in working with asymmetric ciphers is to generate an applicable key pair. Let's look at the JCA's facilities for key pair generation.

3.1 The KeyPairGenerator Engine

Every asymmetric cipher requires a pair of keys before any cryptographic operation can be performed. The responsibility for key generation falls to an engine class, java.security.KeyPairGenerator. As an engine, it implements the standard pair of engine factory methods, for example:

```
KeyPairGenerator kpg = KeyPairGenerator.getInstance("RSA");
```

This engine shares many of the same characteristics of the KeyGenerator covered in Chapter 2, including support for algorithm independent or algorithm specific key generation. Sadly, this is an area where design discrepancies between the JCA and the JCE teams show through. This engine was part of the JCA, and while it still operates with similar initialization concepts to its cousin, the method is spelled out in its entirety—initialize(). Beyond this semantic difference, the four overloaded methods use identical argument signatures and operate in an identical concept to the init() method of the KeyGenerator engine class, previously covered in Chapter 3. If you need a refresher, flip back one chapter and review sections 2.3.1 and 2.3.2.

3.1.1 Code Example: Algorithm Independent Key Pair Generation

Key pair generation requires a minimum of two pieces of information regardless of algorithm type—key size (in bits) and a source of randomness. Like everything else in the JCA/JCE, if the source of randomness is omitted it is the provider's responsibility to obtain that source—-usually through an internal SecureRandom engine. Let's look at a code example:

Example 3.1 Sample Code Location: com.mkp.jce.chap3.GenerateKeyPair

```
1  try
2  {
3      if(args.length == 0)
4      {
5          System.err.println("Usage: java GenerateKeyPair pairName");
6          System.err.println(" Keys are written to the root directory");
7          System.err.println(" with .pubkey and .privkey extensions");
8          System.exit(0);
```

```
9     }

10

11    File pubKeyFile = new File("/" + args[0] + ".pubkey");

12    File privKeyFile = new File("/" + args[0] + ".privkey");

13

14    KeyPairGenerator kpg = KeyPairGenerator.getInstance("RSA");

15    kpg.initialize(1024);

16    KeyPair keyPair = kpg.genKeyPair();

17

18    FileOutputStream publicFos = new FileOutputStream(pubKeyFile);

19    publicFos.write(keyPair.getPublic().getEncoded());

20    publicFos.close();

21

22    FileOutputStream privFos = new FileOutputStream(privKeyFile);

23    privFos.write(keyPair.getPrivate().getEncoded());

24    privFos.close();

25

26 } catch (NoSuchAlgorithmException kpgNsae)

27 {

28    //The RSA key pair generator algorithm couldn't be found

29 } catch (FileNotFoundException fnfe)

30 {

31    //Couldn't find the filename specified

32 } catch (IOException ioe)

33 {

34    //Problems reading or writing the files

35 }
```

The sample assumes that a single argument was provided on the command line that represents the name that should be used when persisting the generated keys. Lines 11 and

12 build the absolute filename path, defaulting to the root. Lines 14 through 16 is responsible for the actual generation of the key pair. On line 15, we specify that we want our key to be 1024-bits in length. The KeyPairGenerator actually produces the keys when the genKeyPair() method is invoked on line 16. As a convenience, the JCA defines a wrapper class KeyPair that offers no real functionality beyond holding onto a single instance of a private key and its corresponding public key. Two convenience methods are defined, getPrivate() and getPublic(), which return the associated PrivateKey and PublicKey instances, respectively. Once we've generated our key pair, we can use them in a digital signature operation (digital signatures are discussed in Chapter 4). If the algorithm supports it, we could also use them in an encryption operation (an example of which is detailed shortly in this chapter).

3.1.2 Comparing Symmetric and Asymmetric Keys

Symmetric ciphers by nature are architected to operate with small key sizes. For example, the dated DES cipher only works with a 56-bit key—a mere 7 bytes. (Of course, the protection level offered by a 56-bit key is very questionable with today's hardware.) More advanced ciphers like AES can use 128-bits, 192-bits, or 256-bits in its key [17], offering a greater degree of protection than a cipher like DES. Regardless of the number of bits, these symmetric secret keys are random in nature.

Asymmetric keys are often 1024-bits or larger. Why the difference? Well, asymmetric ciphers operate on a different internal design principal altogether, with their foundation on math that is (surprising to some) thousands of years old. Let's look at the RSA asymmetric cipher to gain better insight into the composition of a key pair.

Since its introduction in 1977, the RSA algorithm has been based on mathematics known as the *Integer Factorization Problem* (IFP) [18]. The IFP is considered the de facto asymmetric cipher standard. In the spirit of keeping the mathematics here at a high school level, the first step in generating a pair of RSA keys is to compute *n* from the multiplication of two very large prime numbers, *p* and *q*. When we say very large prime numbers, we are talking about *p* and *q* each containing around 308-digits. Now that's a big number! These numbers can be achieved when RSA is initialized using 1024-bits or larger. After *n* is calculated, more mathematic functions are invoked resulting in two additional integers commonly referred to as *t, e* and *d*. The set {p, q, t, d} forms the private key while the set {n, e} forms the public key [16]. While this is probably the most nonmathematical, succinct definition of the RSA cryptosystem you'll find, it is sufficient for discussion here. For those truly interested in delving into the mathematics behind asymmetric ciphers, pick up a copy of *Practical Cryptography* by Ferguson and Schneier (ISBN: 0-471-22357-3) and dive head first into mathematical proofs for prime numbers and elaborate explanations of the Chinese Remainder Theorem! If an attacker only knows the smaller set of numbers exposed by the public key, mathematically speaking it is incredibly difficult to compute (in any reasonable amount of time) the corresponding set of numbers that comprise the private key. This explains why an RSA private key (when stored to disk for example) is larger than the public key in size—there's more information to track. Large prime numbers make this operation successful and ensure that attackers who want to try and compute the private key from only the two known public key numbers should block off the next couple of centuries on their calendar even if they are using today's super computers.

3.1.3   Persisting a Key: Key Encodings Defined

All of our work with symmetric ciphers used simplistic byte[] secret keys. In addition to the secret keys, some symmetric cipher examples in Chapter 2 used initialization vectors when certain cipher modes were selected, but the IV was completely separate from the secret key. When it came time to preserve the symmetric cipher key, for example by persisting it out to the file system, we simply wrote out the raw bytes—there was no encoding applied to the key since it was, well, literally just raw bytes randomly generated, and we recorded the IV somewhere for future use. However, as we've seen, asymmetric keys include much more information than an array of randomly generated bytes. Asymmetric key pairs are actually comprised of sets of related numbers that are plugged into advanced mathematical formulas. To retain provider independence, it is essential that when we persist either of the asymmetric keys we do so using a standardized format. Public keys rely on an encoding format known as X.509. (Digital certificates use this same encoding, and we work with them in Chapter 5.) Private keys rely on an encoding format known as PKCS#8. Let's now look at a code sample that verifies this information.

3.1.4   Code Example: Inspecting Key Encodings

This code example generates keys from several well-known algorithms, including DES, Password Based Encryption, and RSA. We're going to look at the meta-data available from the Key interface that tells us about the algorithm and the encoding format that will be returned when a Key instance responds to a getEncoded() method invocation.

Example 3.2 Sample Code Location: com.mkp.jce.chap3.KeyEncodingSampler

```
1  byte[] salt = new byte[] { (byte) 0x3a, (byte)0x44, (byte)0x7f, (byte)0xf1,
2                              (byte)0xa2, (byte)0xe5, (byte)0x87, (byte)0x31 };
3  int iterations = 25;
4
5  try
6  {
7      char[] password = new char[] { 's', 'e', 'c', 'r', 'e', 't' };
8
```

```
9       PBEKeySpec pbeKeySpec = new PBEKeySpec(password, salt, iterations);
10      SecretKeyFactory factory =
11            SecretKeyFactory.getInstance("PBEWithMD5AndDES");
12      SecretKey pbeKey = factory.generateSecret(pbeKeySpec);
13      System.out.println("Key Algorithm: " + pbeKey.getAlgorithm());
14      System.out.println("\tKey Encoding: " + pbeKey.getFormat());
15
16      KeyGenerator kg = KeyGenerator.getInstance("DES");
17      SecretKey desKey = kg.generateKey();
18      System.out.println("Key Algorithm: " + desKey.getAlgorithm());
19      System.out.println("\tKey Encoding: " + desKey.getFormat());
20
21      KeyPairGenerator kpg = KeyPairGenerator.getInstance("RSA");
22      kpg.initialize(1024);
23      KeyPair keyPair = kpg.generateKeyPair();
24
25      PublicKey pubKey = keyPair.getPublic();
26
27      System.out.println("Public Key Algorithm: " + pubKey.getAlgorithm());
28      System.out.println("\tKey Encoding: " + pubKey.getFormat());
29
30      PrivateKey privKey = keyPair.getPrivate();
31      System.out.println("Private Key Algorithm: " + privKey.getAlgorithm());
32      System.out.println("\tKey Encoding: " + privKey.getFormat());
33
34 } catch (NoSuchAlgorithmException nsae)
35 {
36    //Oops- one of the requested algorithms wasn't available
37 } catch (InvalidKeySpecException ike)
38 {
```

```
39    //The key specification was invalid
40 }
```

At this point, we've covered the usage of each engine included in this code sample. Our interest here is the result of the various System.out statements that provide insight into the key encoding. Here's the output from this sample:

```
Key Algorithm: PBEWithMD5AndDES
        Key Encoding: RAW
Key Algorithm: DES
        Key Encoding: RAW
Public Key Algorithm: RSA
        Key Encoding: X509
Private Key Algorithm: RSA
        Key Encoding: PKCS8
```

We can see that the password-based encryption and DES apply no encoding to their secret keys; they are just raw byte arrays. We also see that different encoding formats are applied to each key in the asymmetric key pair. It's beyond our scope to discuss the physical formats of PKCS#8 and X.509, but knowing the existence of these encoding schemes is a must to successfully read and write asymmetric key pairs.

Chapter 2 (section 2.4 specifically) introduced us to the KeySpec marker interface. This interface was important because it symbolized a transparent key specification. Recall that our use of *transparent* here means that the key's meta-data is accessible and visible. By describing the key in a provider-neutral format, the JCA supports situations where an instance of a KeyPairGenerator engine could be from *Provider A*, and an instance of a Cipher engine could be from *Provider B*. This architecture allowed the downstream developers (you and me) to mix and match providers throughout the process as we saw fit. We also stated that providers could implement this interface to produce key algorithm specific definitions with methods that exposed meta-data pertinent to that type of key. Chapter 2 also demonstrated an example of the DESKeySpec that determines if a weak or semi-weak key was used. The JCA includes two more implementations specifically for use with public and private key encoding formats:

- java.security.spec.PKCS8EncodedKeySpec
- java.security.spec.X509EncodedKeySpec

The PKCS8EncodedKeySpec is used to load a PKCS#8 encoded private key, while the X509EncodedKeySpec loads an X.509 encoded public key. Invocation of the getEncoded()

method on any Key instance automatically returns a byte array properly encoded for that key type. Each provider is required to document which key specifications they support for a given cipher, so be sure to review your provider's documentation for further details. Let's look at some examples of how to read X.509 encoded public keys and PKCS#8 encoded private keys.

3.1.5 Code Example: Loading an X.509 Encoded Public Key from Disk

Earlier in the chapter, the GenerateKeyPair code example wrote out its generated public key and private key to disk. Using our newfound knowledge of encoding formats, let's look at how we can recover the X.509 encoded public key. Since the public key is, well, public, there is no need to protect it. We could send the file as written to anyone, perhaps via e-mail. Any software package that knows how to read X.509 encoded public keys would be able to load and use the public key in a cipher or signature verification operation.

Example 3.3 Sample Code Location: com.mkp.jce.chap3.LoadPublicKey

```
1   ByteArrayOutputStream privKeyBaos = new ByteArrayOutputStream();

2

3   try

4   {

5       //Be sure to copy the jcebook.privkey to your working directory

6       //or change to an absolute path to ensure the files found

7       FileInputStream privKeyFis = new FileInputStream(

8                                         new File("/jcebook.privkey"));

9

10      int curByte=0;

11      while( (curByte = privKeyFis.read()) != -1 )

12      {

13              privKeyBaos.write(curByte);

14      }

15

16      X509EncodedKeySpec keySpec =

17              new X509EncodedKeySpec(pubKeyBaos.toByteArray());

18      pubKeyBaos.close();
```

```
19      KeyFactory keyFactoryEngine = KeyFactory.getInstance("RSA");

20      PrivateKey privateKey = keyFactoryEngine.generatePrivate(keySpec);

21      System.out.println("Private Key Successfully Loaded!");

22 } catch (IOException ioe)

23 {

24      //Handle This!

25 } catch (NoSuchAlgorithmException nsae)

26 {

27      //Handle This!

28 } catch (InvalidKeySpecException ikse)

29 {

30      //Handle This!

31 }
```

For those rusty in their Java I/O operations, this code sample (and the next to read a private key) relies on the powerful ByteArrayOutputStream class. While termed an output stream, the bytes are in essence written only to memory, making it easy to read an arbitrarily sized file and easily gain access to the data as a byte[] through the toByteArray() method. We open up the file and read in the bytes on lines 7 through 14. Once we've read the whole file, we create a new instance of an X509EncodedKeySpec from the byte array produced by the ByteArrayOutputStream class on lines 16 and 17. With the transparent key specification in hand, we request an instance of an RSA KeyFactory and on line 20 ask the KeyFactory to turn our encoded public key into a PublicKey instance. At this point, we can hand that key over to an instance of a Cipher engine to perform encryption or decryption or even pass it to an instance of a Signature engine to verify a digital signature of a document.

3.1.6   Code Example: Loading a PKCS#8 Encoded Private Key from Disk

Reading a PKCS#8 encoded private key differs only in the physical KeySpec implementation used, PKCS8EncodedKeySpec.

Example 3.4 Sample Code Location: com.mkp.jce.chap3.LoadPrivateKey

```
1  ByteArrayOutputStream privKeyBaos = new ByteArrayOutputStream();

2
```

```
3  try
4  {
5      //Be sure to copy the jcebook.privkey to your working directory
6      //or change to an absolute path to ensure the files found
7      FileInputStream privKeyFis = new FileInputStream(
8                                  new File("/jcebook.privkey"));
9
10     int curByte=0;
11     while( (curByte = privKeyFis.read()) != -1 )
12     {
13             privKeyBaos.write(curByte);
14     }
15
16     PKCS8EncodedKeySpec keySpec =
17                 new PKCS8EncodedKeySpec(privKeyBaos.toByteArray());
18     privKeyBaos.close();
19     KeyFactory keyFactoryEngine = KeyFactory.getInstance("RSA");
20     PrivateKey privateKey = keyFactoryEngine.generatePrivate(keySpec);
21     System.out.println("Private Key Successfully Loaded!");
22 } catch (IOException ioe)
23 {
24     //Handle This!
25 } catch (NoSuchAlgorithmException nsae)
26 {
27     //Handle This!
28 } catch (InvalidKeySpecException ikse)
29 {
30     //Handle This!
31 }
```

We can see the algorithms are nearly identical. We modified the name of the file to load (jcebook.privkey), switched to a PKCS8EncodedKeySpec instance and requested the KeyFactory to decode and deliver an instance of a PrivateKey from the encoded bytes. In Chapter 5, we are going to discuss the use of a key store to manage our keys. Realistically, we wouldn't want to leave our private key on the hard drive in the open.

Now that we have a firm grasp on generating, reading, and writing asymmetric cipher key pairs, we are ready to revisit the Cipher engine and see an asymmetric cipher in action.

3.2   Revisiting the Cipher Engine

As previously noted, the Cipher class serves as the entry point into all of the JCE cipher algorithms, relying on the use of the standard pair of engine factory methods. While not every asymmetric cipher supports encryption, this section will use an RSA algorithm, which does. After learning the nomenclature for looking up symmetric ciphers, looking up an asymmetric cipher should be a trivial operation. (If you ever need to look up the algorithm names supported by a provider, remember that the code example CompleteEngineListing in Chapter 1 is very useful for seeing base and aliased names.) Consider this example:

```
Cipher cipher = Cipher.getInstance("RSA/ECB/PKCS1Padding");
```

The invocation of the getInstance() factory method is requesting an RSA asymmetric cipher that employs an ECB cipher mode and a PKCS #1 padding scheme. For a review on cipher modes and padding, flip back to Chapter 2, section 2.6. The factory method will search the java.security file (typically cached) in order of provider preference and any dynamically registered providers. The factory is looking for a provider that supports an implementation of the requested type. Once located, the factory returns an instance of a Cipher class capable of performing the requested work. Initialization and encryption/decryption operations are identical to the symmetric cipher examples found in Chapter 2:

```
cipher.init(Cipher.ENCRYPT_MODE, rsaKeyPair.getPublic());

cipher.doFinal(plainTextString.getBytes());
```

The only noticeable difference is on the init() method. We are still passing in an instance of a Key, however, we have to choose which part of the key pair will be used for the operation. Since this is an encryption operation, we most likely would be using someone else's public key to facilitate transmission of the cipher text over to them. Let's look at an example that encrypts a file with a public key.

3.2.1   Code Example: Encrypting a File with a Public Key

Generally, asymmetric cipher encryption follows strict mechanics—use the recipient's public key to encrypt the data you are going to send them, and they in turn would use your public key to encrypt the data they are going to send you. Let's explore what the SunJCE provider offers in terms of cipher algorithms. The following list is produced from the CompleteEngineListing sample introduced in Chapter 1:

> SunJCE formally supports the following implementations for the Cipher engine :
>
> **Blowfish** as implemented in class com.sun.crypto.provider.BlowfishCipher
>
> **DES** as implemented in class com.sun.crypto.provider.DESCipher
>
> **DESede** as implemented in class com.sun.crypto.provider.DESedeCipher
>
> **DESede** is also aliased to the name TripleDES
>
> **PBEWithMD5AndDES** as implemented in class
>
> com.sun.crypto.provider.PBEWithMD5AndDESCipher
>
> **PBEWithMD5AndTripleDES** as implemented in class
>
> com.sun.crypto.provider.PBEWithMD5AndTripleDESCipher

This listing shows that neither RSA nor any other asymmetric ciphers that support encryption are available through the SunJCE provider. There is no need to explore the SUN provider (which came with the JCA) because the Cipher engine wasn't introduced until the JCE was released. Both the Bouncy Castle ("BC") and the Cryptix ("CryptixCrypto") open source providers offer RSA asymmetric cipher solutions. Let's look at a code example that dynamically registers these additional JCE providers and then encrypts a sample text file using RSA/ECB/PKCS1Padding. Prior to running this example, be sure to create a new plaintext file named message.txt on the root (either at / or c:\) or adjust the code to read from your home directly. The sample message.txt included with the source code merely reads:

> The quick brown fox jumps over the lazy dog

Example 3.5 Sample Code Location: com.mkp.jce.chap3.PublicKeyEncryption

```
1  try
2  {
3      Provider bcProv =
4              new org.bouncycastle.jce.provider.BouncyCastleProvider();
5      Security.insertProviderAt(bcProv, 5);
6
7      Provider cryptixProv =
8              new cryptix.jce.provider.CryptixCrypto();
9      Security.insertProviderAt(cryptixProv, 6);
```

```
10
11     //Load the public key saved from the GenerateKeyPair code example
12     PublicKey pubKey =
13            CryptoUtil.loadPublicKey(new File("/jcebook.pubkey"), "RSA");
14
15     //Locate an RSA cipher engine; init using pub key for encryption
16     Cipher cipher = Cipher.getInstance("RSA/ECB/PKCS1Padding");
17     cipher.init(Cipher.ENCRYPT_MODE, pubKey);
18
19     String plainText =
20            CryptoUtil.readPlainTextFile(new File("/message.txt"));
21
22     byte[] cipherText = cipher.doFinal(plainText.getBytes());
23
24     CryptoUtil.writeCipherTextFile(new File("/ciphertext.dat"), cipherText);
25 } catch (IOException ioe)
26 {
27     //Oops- can't read the file
28 } catch (NoSuchAlgorithmException nsae)
29 {
30     //Hmmm- looks like the dynamic registration may not have worked
31 } catch (InvalidKeySpecException ikse)
32 {
33     //The key specification was invalid
34 } catch (NoSuchPaddingException nspe)
35 {
36     //The requested padding isn't available
37 } catch (InvalidKeyException ike)
38 {
39     //The key was invalid
```

```
40 } catch (IllegalStateException ise)
41 {
42    //Can't do that!
43 } catch (IllegalBlockSizeException ibse)
44 {
45    //The block size was too big
46 } catch (BadPaddingException bpe)
47 {
48    //The padding was incorrect
49 }
```

This example dynamically registers the Bouncy Castle and the Cryptix JCE providers in lines 3 through 9. The primary benefit of dynamic registration is that we don't have to modify the java.security file. On lines 12 and 13 we load the PublicKey that was generated from a previous example in this chapter. Line 16 requests our RSA asymmetric cipher, and on line 17 we initialize the RSA instance using the public key. Overall, the only difference between symmetric and asymmetric cipher operations with the Cipher engine is that we pass either the public or private key. Let's look at how the ciphertext can be decrypted using the private key.

3.2.2 Code Example: Decrypting a File with a Private Key

There is only one major difference between the encryption and decryption process with an asymmetric cipher engine—we must use the private key for decryption operations, initializing the Cipher engine in Cipher.DECRYPT_MODE.

Example 3.6 Sample Code Location: com.mkp.jce.chap3.PrivateKeyDecryption

```
1  try
2  {
3      Provider bcProv =
4            new org.bouncycastle.jce.provider.BouncyCastleProvider();
5      Security.insertProviderAt(bcProv, 5);
6
```

```
7    Provider cryptixProv =
8            new cryptix.jce.provider.CryptixCrypto();
9    Security.insertProviderAt(cryptixProv, 6);
10
11   //Be sure to verify jcebook.privkey is on root
12   FileInputStream privKeyFis =
13           new FileInputStream(new File("/jcebook.privkey"));
14
15   ByteArrayOutputStream baos = new ByteArrayOutputStream();
16
17   int curByte=0;
18   while( (curByte = privKeyFis.read()) != -1 )
19   {
20           baos.write(curByte);
21   }
22
23   PKCS8EncodedKeySpec keySpec =
24           new PKCS8EncodedKeySpec(baos.toByteArray());
25   baos.close();
26
27   KeyFactory keyFactoryEngine = KeyFactory.getInstance("RSA");
28   PrivateKey privateKey = keyFactoryEngine.generatePrivate(keySpec);
29
30   Cipher cipher = Cipher.getInstance("RSA/ECB/PKCS1Padding");
31   cipher.init(Cipher.DECRYPT_MODE, privateKey);
32
33   byte[] cipherText =
34           CryptoUtil.readCipherTextFile(new File("/ciphertext.dat"));
35
36   String plainText = new String(cipher.doFinal(cipherText));
37   System.out.println("Decrypted:\n" + plainText);
```

```
38
39 } catch (IOException ioe)
40 {
41    //Oops- can't read the file
42 } catch (NoSuchAlgorithmException nsae)
43 {
44    //Hmmm- looks like the dynamic registration may not have worked
45 } catch (InvalidKeySpecException ikse)
46 {
47    //The key specification was invalid
48 } catch (NoSuchPaddingException nspe)
49 {
50    //The requested padding isn't available
51 } catch (InvalidKeyException ike)
52 {
53    //The key was invalid
54 } catch (IllegalStateException ise)
55 {
56    //Can't do that!
57 } catch (IllegalBlockSizeException ibse)
58 {
59    //The block was too big
60 } catch (BadPaddingException bpe)
61 {
62    //The padding was incorrect
63 }
```

Lines 11 through 28 are used to load our PKCS#8 encoded private key from the example earlier in this chapter. In Chapter 5, we will talk about the KeyStore and how we can use one to manage our key pairs in a more acceptable manner. Once we have obtained an instance of a PrivateKey, we initialize our asymmetric cipher in decrypt mode on line 31, passing in the private key. From this point forward, decryption works identically to that of a symmetric cipher.

3.3   Comparing Keys for Equality

A provider will typically offer a well designed solution that properly implements the equals(), hashcode() and clone() methods, as well as implement the java.io.Serializable interface. In the event you need to determine key equality and the equals() method isn't implemented by the provider, the best way to determine key equality is to simply compare the keys byte-by-byte. Instead of looping, use the java.util.Arrays helper class:

```
boolean identKeys = (Arrays.equals(key1.getEncoded(), key2.getEncoded());
```

In the event the keys that require comparison are in different formats, for example one is of type RSAPrivateKey and the other is from a certificate represented by RSAPrivateCrtKey, then you should consider comparing the individual data parts to determine equality:

```
boolean identKeys = (privKey.getModulus().equals(privCrtKey.getModulus()) &&

        privKey.getPrivateExponent().equals(privCrtKey.getPrivateExponent()));
```

We'll formally introduce digital certificates in Chapter 5.

3.4   Looking to the Future: Elliptic Curve Cryptography

In 1985, a newer approach to public key cryptography was proposed, based on the mathematics in the *Elliptic Curve Discrete Logarithm Problem* (ECDLP) [18]. Let's look at the key generation process, again keeping with the spirit of brevity. An elliptic curve *E* is selected with a number of points on it and is divisible by a large number, *n*. A point *q* on the curve is selected, and a random point *d* is identified in the range of *1* through *n − 1*. This value *d* forms the private key. Another variable *p* is calculated as the result of *dq,* and the set {E,p,n,q} represents the public key.

 Why cover this information, especially at such a high level? One conclusion we can draw that differentiates ECC over RSA is the minimum computational requirements to generate the keys. Section 3.1.2 alludes to the fact that RSA is working with 308-digit integers and performing exponential operations against such large numbers. Clearly, the computational overhead involved with these types of mathematical operations are huge. Today, there are few (if any) mobile devices (PDA's, Cell Phones, etc.) that are prepared to handle mathematical operations that involve such large numbers. Comparitively, ECC encryption relies on the simple formula np=q where *p* and *q* are points on the curve. Remembering that multiplication can be substituted with addition (adding p, n times), and that the data points on the curve serve as the muscle in the equation, the computation cost is extremely low compared to RSA and thus suitable for traditional (desktop PCs, for example) as well as mobile devices. Mathematicians would also agree that the ECDLP is significantly harder to solve than the IFP that is used by RSA. In fact, consider what are mathematically equivalent keys in terms of strength: 160-bit ECC key and a 1024-bit RSA key.

ECC shows great promise, offering the same level of security as RSA but using much smaller keys. The jury is still out, and some mathematicians feel that ECC hasn't been studied hard enough and that a simple mechanism to crack the math exists. To put this in perspective, if anyone figured out easier solutions to either the IFP or the ECDLP, the encrypted documents that exist today immediately become obsolete.

Today, JDK 1.4 doesn't directly offer any ECC algorithms, though some third party providers may offer ECC solutions. At JavaOne 2003, there was a security session entitled "J2SE Security Looks Ahead: New Features from Cryptography to XML Security" that was hosted by two members of Sun's security team. One of the speculations made (since there wasn't even a JDK 1.5 beta available at the time of writing, I have to use the word speculation) is that JDK 1.5 will include better support for ECC.

3.4.1 Asymmetric Cipher Wrap-up

In Chapter 2, the `Cipher` engine was discussed in great detail with regard to symmetric cryptography. As we've seen, this engine's architecture is extremely robust and flexible, easily extending support for asymmetric ciphers. Most of the details in performing asymmetric cipher operations lie in working with the public and private keys and their respective encodings. Once an instance of the appropriate key is loaded and in its usable form (`PublicKey` or `PrivateKey` instance), the `Cipher` engine's functionality and operation requires no real knowledge about what type of cipher algorithm—symmetric or asymmetric—is being employed.

3.5 **The** `KeyAgreement` **Engine**

The mathematic theories that define asymmetric encryption are very powerful. In fact, these mathematical characteristics can be used to solve a common problem: identifying a shared secret key between two or more parties without any party having to formally divulge the specific secret key over a public channel. This is particularly advantageous over a symmetric cipher only implementation, which would require that the parties somehow correspond to ensure they each are using identical keys. It also is an advantageous design when you may be contacted by an anonymous party whom you've neither previously exchanged public keys, nor do you intend to keep a copy of their public key, but you want a secure conversation.

Alice and Bob want to carry on a secure conversation, but they are unable to meet face to face to discuss what key should be used in their symmetric cipher engines to protect their content. We know that the security of any cipher lies in the cipher algorithm itself, and even if an attacker obtains knowledge of what cipher is being used, the cipher-text isn't compromised unless the key is lost. Alice and Bob exchange e-mails and phone calls, ultimately deciding on a handshaking protocol and a symmetric cipher to use once they establish a secure channel between them. Bob agrees to be the server that listens for requests from Alice, who will act as the client. They will rely on a Diffie-Hellman key exchange protocol, often referred to simply as *DH*, to establish a shared secret. Unbe-knownst to either Alice or Bob, Eve plans on intercepting Alice's outbound TCP/IP traffic, printing it out to the screen to listen in on the conversation, and then forwarding the request onto Bob. Eve's actions are often referred to as a *Man in the Middle Attack* because Eve could theoretically attempt to attack the message and change it before forwarding it on to Bob. Eve will relay Bob's response back to Alice, once again after printing out the text to the screen and again theoretically have the opportunity to change the meaning of the message. Despite this blatant *Man in the Middle* attack by Eve, Alice and Bob's conversation will remain secure because they will never have to explicitly send their secret key over the network, leaving Eve in the dark even if she managed to intercept what cipher algorithm was being employed.

> NOTE: The following code examples rely on several Java I/O concepts that are new with JDK 1.4. If you are unfamiliar with the `java.nio.*` package, take a look at the code examples and documentation guides that are included with the J2SE 1.4.1 SDK. Here you will find substantial JavaDocs and several code examples that demonstrate a `TimeServer` using classes and concepts similar to our examples.

3.5.1 Code Example: Key Exchange to Establish a Secure Channel

In this code example, we see Bob establishing a server to wait for a request from Alice (act-ing as the client) to initiate a secure conversation. The establishment of the secure channel will come from the Diffie-Hellman key exchange protocol. Alice and Bob agreed on the Hello/Bye-Bye handshaking protocol seen in the code example ahead of time. Essentially, the protocol is as follows:

1. Alice sends Bob's server a *Hello* message

2. Bob responds back with a *Hello* message to indicate he is ready to proceed

3. Alice generates an encoded DH public key and forwards to Bob

4. Bob, using Alice's encoded DH public key, generates his encoded DH public key and replies back to Alice, forwarding his encoded DH public key

5. With keys exchanged, Alice and Bob calculate their common shared secret

6. Alice sends Bob an encrypted message using, for example, DES/ECB/PKCS8Padding keyed off of the shared secret

7. Bob receives the ciphertext and decrypts it, responding back to Alice with an encrypted response using the same cipher algorithm

8. Alice decrypts the response and ends the conversation by sending a *Bye-Bye* message

9. Bob acknowledges the end of the conversation by responding with a *Bye-Bye* message of his own

This is arguably the most complex set of code examples found in this book. The reason is that any key exchange implementation requires at least two parties. We've also added in Eve as a *Man in the Middle* attacker, bringing our program count up to three. We'll first talk about Alice's client and Bob's server and how they generate their shared secret key. The areas of the code examples that we'll be discussing have a 15% shade applied to them, and in their top-right corner we've labeled them using A or B, for Alice or Bob, respectively, and added a sequence number. This approach makes it easy to jump back and forth between the applications. After we understand these two programs, we'll introduce Eve in the middle and look at the output she was able to extract from listening in our pair.

Our focus is on cryptography, not Java I/O or the functionality found in the new `java.nio.*` package. As such, we will restrict our conversations to only those aspects of the program that establish the exchanged secret keys. Additionally, you should note that the actual messages being exchanged throughout the example has been encoded to UTF-8, for example, `myStringVar.getBytes("UTF-8")`. It is especially important to keep encoding issues in mind when developing large geographically distributed applications and for all parties to reach consensus on which encoding to use.

Key exchange requires knowledge for all of the material leading up to this point. Because we are talking about different machines and thus different JVMs, the first thing you'll notice is that we have to use algorithm specific initialization, using the `AlgorithmParameterGenerator` engine and several classes that implement the `AlgorithmParameterSpec` marker interface to ensure type safety throughout our process.

Example 3.7 Sample Code Location: com.mkp.jce.chap3.AliceClient

```
try
{
    InetSocketAddress isa =
            new InetSocketAddress(InetAddress.getLocalHost(), 8787);
    SocketChannel sc = SocketChannel.open();
    sc.connect(isa);

    try
    {
        System.out.println("Creating DH parameters (be patient!)...");
```

```
A1    AlgorithmParameterGenerator paramGen =
            AlgorithmParameterGenerator.getInstance("DH");
      paramGen.init(512);
      AlgorithmParameters params = paramGen.generateParameters();


      DHParameterSpec dhSkipParamSpec =
            (DHParameterSpec) params.getParameterSpec(DHParameterSpec.class);
```

```
      System.out.println("Generating a DH KeyPair...");
```

```
A2    KeyPairGenerator aliceKpairGen = KeyPairGenerator.getInstance("DH");
      aliceKpairGen.initialize(dhSkipParamSpec);
      KeyPair aliceKpair = aliceKpairGen.generateKeyPair();
```

```
      System.out.println("Initializing DH KeyAgreement Engine w/private key");
```

```
A3    KeyAgreement aliceKeyAgree = KeyAgreement.getInstance("DH");
      aliceKeyAgree.init(aliceKpair.getPrivate());
      byte[] alicePubKeyEnc = aliceKpair.getPublic().getEncoded();
```

```
      System.out.println("Sending Hello");
      ByteBuffer helloBuf = ByteBuffer.wrap("Hello\n".getBytes("UTF-8"));
      int sent = sc.write(helloBuf);


      String response = new String(CryptoUtil.readFromSocketChannel(sc));
      System.out.print("Response: " + response);


      System.out.println("Sending my encoded public key- " +
                  alicePubKeyEnc.length + " bytes");
      ByteBuffer encodedCert = ByteBuffer.wrap(alicePubKeyEnc);
      sent = sc.write(encodedCert);
```

```
A4    byte[] bobPubKeyEnc = CryptoUtil.readFromSocketChannel(sc);

      System.out.println("Response: Bob's Encoded Public Key: " +
                  bobPubKeyEnc.length + " bytes");


A5    KeyFactory aliceKeyFac = KeyFactory.getInstance("DH");
      X509EncodedKeySpec x509KeySpec =
                  new X509EncodedKeySpec(bobPubKeyEnc);
      PublicKey bobPubKey = aliceKeyFac.generatePublic(x509KeySpec);

      System.out.println("Executing PHASE1 of key agreement...");


A6    aliceKeyAgree.doPhase(bobPubKey, true);
      byte[] aliceSharedSecret = aliceKeyAgree.generateSecret();

      System.out.println("Alice secret (DEBUG ONLY):" +
                  CryptoUtil.toHexString(aliceSharedSecret));


      // The previous invocation of generateSecret() reset the key
      // agreement object, so we call doPhase again prior to another
      // generateSecret call

A7    aliceKeyAgree.doPhase(bobPubKey, true);
      SecretKey aliceDesKey = aliceKeyAgree.generateSecret("DES");

      Cipher aliceCipher = Cipher.getInstance("DES/ECB/PKCS5Padding");
      aliceCipher.init(Cipher.ENCRYPT_MODE, aliceDesKey);

      byte[] plaintext = "Go Buckeyes!".getBytes("UTF-8");
      byte[] ciphertext = aliceCipher.doFinal(plaintext);

      System.out.println("Sending encrypted message");
```

```
        ByteBuffer cipherBuf = ByteBuffer.wrap(ciphertext);
        sent = sc.write(cipherBuf);


        byte[] recoveredPlaintext = CryptoUtil.readFromSocketChannel(sc);


        aliceCipher.init(Cipher.DECRYPT_MODE, aliceDesKey);
        String recovered = new String(aliceCipher.doFinal(recoveredPlaintext));


        System.out.println("Decrypted Message: " + recovered);


        System.out.println("Sending Bye-Bye");
        ByteBuffer byebyeBuf = ByteBuffer.wrap("Bye-Bye\n".getBytes("UTF-8"));
        sc.write(byebyeBuf);
        sc.close();


} catch (NoSuchAlgorithmException e)
{
    e.printStackTrace();
} catch (InvalidKeySpecException e)
{
    e.printStackTrace();
} catch (InvalidKeyException e)
{
    e.printStackTrace();
} catch (IllegalStateException e)
{
    e.printStackTrace();
} catch (InvalidParameterSpecException e)
{
    e.printStackTrace();
```

```
    } catch (InvalidAlgorithmParameterException e)
    {
       e.printStackTrace();
    } catch (NoSuchPaddingException e)
    {
       e.printStackTrace();
    } catch (IllegalBlockSizeException e)
    {
       e.printStackTrace();
    } catch (BadPaddingException e)
    {
       e.printStackTrace();
    } finally
    {
       // Make sure we close the channel (and hence the socket)
       if (sc != null) sc.close();
    }
} catch (IOException ioe)
{
   ioe.printStackTrace();
}
```

Alice's view of the complete conversation is pictured in Figure 3.1. In **A1** we can see Alice initiate the Diffie-Hellman key exchange by obtaining an instance of an AlgorithmParameterGenerator. This is the first time we've seen this engine in use. Essentially, the engine generates a full set of parameters required for a given operation through a single method invocation. Diffie-Hellman only requires two parameters to initiate the key exchange process. The first parameter is the size of the prime modulus, while the second parameter is the size of the random exponent (both in bits). Alice indicates that the engine should be initialized using 512-bits of random data. Since no source of randomness was supplied, the highest priority installed provider's SecureRandom class will be used. Once the engine is initialized, an invocation of the generateParameters() method is made. In our case,

```
wiseman in ~/Desktop/Morgan-Kaufmann/src/bin (11)--> java com.mkp.jce.chap4.AliceClient
Creating DH parameters (be patient!)...
Generating a DH KeyPair...
Initializing the KeyAgreement Engine with DH private key
Sending Hello
Response: Hello
Sending my encoded public key- 226 bytes
Response: Bob's Encoded Public Key: 226 bytes
Executing PHASE1 of key agreement...
Alice secret (DEBUG ONLY):1D:04:8F:36:76:E5:3D:A8:86:B1:76:9A:52:99:8D:0E:B0:DE:9C:67:89:8
D:57:B6:40:0C:E2:A5:40:19:99:89:28:7C:5E:7F:E9:EF:30:BC:D5:37:CA:4E:65:21:47:83:95:6D:CF:D
9:3D:36:47:A0:4E:CF:75:C4:29:CD:AB:49
Sending encrypted message
Decrypted Message: Beat Michigan!
Sending Bye-Bye
Done.
wiseman in ~/Desktop/Morgan-Kaufmann/src/bin (12)-->
```

Figure 3.1: Alice's screen.

the AlgorithmParameterGenerator requested was for DH (Diffie-Hellman). The output of the generateParameters() method is an opaque representation of all of the parameters necessary to complete a DH exchange in the form of an AlgorithmParameters instance. To access individual parameters transparently, we invoke the getParameterSpec() method, passing in the class of the parameter we want to obtain. The last line of code in the **A1** block extracts a DHParameterSpec (DH for Diffie-Hellman).

Symmetric ciphers typically only required a single piece of data—the key that should be used in the encryption or decryption operation. As a result, there is little use for the combination of the AlgorithmParameterGenerator and the AlgorithmParameters classes in the symmetric cipher world. The more complex asymmetric ciphers you work with, the higher the probability that you will find yourself using this class combination to setup the asymmetric environment.

In **A2**, we obtain a KeyPairGenerator. This was the first engine we discussed in this chapter. In this case, a DH generator instance is requested, and it is initialized using the DHParameterSpec instance. By using the algorithm specific initialization of the KeyPair-Generator, we pass a single instance of DHParameterSpec class. Remember, all classes that implement the ParameterSpec marker interface are considered transparent parameters. When the DH generator receives the DHParameterSpec it can invoke the getter methods of the class to pull out the parameters required to formally generate the KeyPair, which is the last operation in the **A2** block.

Finally, with the DH keys in hand, the **A3** block requests an instance of the Key-Agreement engine. This engine specifically works with key exchange algorithms, like DH. After obtaining a DH instance of the engine, it is initialized using Alice's private key. We won't use this engine again until after we receive Bob's DH public key. For that to occur, we have to send Bob Alice's public key, which we extract in an X.509 encoding scheme and

```
┌─ 000 ──────── Wiseman's World — bash (ttyp1) — ⌘1 ──────────┐
│ wiseman in ~/Desktop/Morgan-Kaufmann/src/bin (8)--> java com.mkp.jce.chap4.BobServer  │
│ Waiting for Alice's call...                                                           │
│ Received: Hello                                                                       │
│ Sending Hello Back                                                                    │
│ Received Alice's Encoded Public Key: 226 bytes                                        │
│ Sending my Encoded Public Key                                                         │
│ Generate DH keypair ...                                                               │
│ Initializing KeyAgreement engine...                                                   │
│ Sending Encoded Public Key~ 226 bytes                                                 │
│ Execute PHASE1 ...                                                                    │
│ Shared secret (DEBUG ONLY): 1D:04:8F:36:76:E5:3D:A8:86:B1:76:9A:52:99:8D:0E:B0:DE:9C:67:89 │
│ :8D:57:B6:40:0C:E2:A5:40:19:99:89:28:7C:5E:7F:E9:EF:30:BC:D5:37:CA:4E:65:21:47:83:95:6D:CF │
│ :D9:3D:36:47:A0:4E:CF:75:C4:29:CD:AB:49                                                │
│ Decrypted Message: Go Buckeyes!                                                        │
│ Sending encrypted response                                                            │
│ Received: Bye-Bye                                                                     │
│ Done                                                                                  │
│ wiseman in ~/Desktop/Morgan-Kaufmann/src/bin (9)--> _                                 │
└────────────────────────────────────────────────────────────┘
```

Figure 3.2: Bob's screen.

broadcast over to Bob in the clear. Now let's see how Bob uses Alice's encoded public key. Bob's view of the complete conversation is pictured in Figure 3.2.

Example 3.8 Sample Code Location: com.mkp.jce.chap3.BobServer

```java
try
{
    System.out.println("Waiting for Alice's call...");

    ServerSocketChannel ssc = ServerSocketChannel.open();
    InetSocketAddress isa =
        new InetSocketAddress(InetAddress.getLocalHost(), 8888);
    ssc.socket().bind(isa);
    SocketChannel sc = ssc.accept();

    try
    {
        String response = new String(CryptoUtil.readFromSocketChannel(sc));
        System.out.print("Received: " + response);
```

```
System.out.println("Sending Hello Back");
ByteBuffer helloBuf = ByteBuffer.wrap("Hello\n".getBytes("UTF-8"));
int sent = sc.write(helloBuf);
```

B1
```
byte[] alicePubKeyEnc = CryptoUtil.readFromSocketChannel(sc);
```
```
System.out.println("Received Alice's Encoded Public Key: " +
            alicePubKeyEnc.length + " bytes");
```

```
System.out.println("Sending my Encoded Public Key");
```

B2
```
KeyFactory bobKeyFac = KeyFactory.getInstance("DH");
X509EncodedKeySpec x509KeySpec =
            New X509EncodedKeySpec(alicePubKeyEnc);
PublicKey alicePubKey = bobKeyFac.generatePublic(x509KeySpec);
DHParameterSpec dhParamSpec = ((DHPublicKey) alicePubKey).getParams();
```

```
System.out.println("Generate DH keypair ...");
```

B3
```
KeyPairGenerator bobKpairGen = KeyPairGenerator.getInstance("DH");
BobKpairGen.initialize(dhParamSpec);
KeyPair bobKpair = bobKpairGen.generateKeyPair();
```

```
System.out.println("Initializing KeyAgreement engine...");
```

B4
```
KeyAgreement bobKeyAgree = KeyAgreement.getInstance("DH");
BobKeyAgree.init(bobKpair.getPrivate());
Byte[] bobPubKeyEnc = bobKpair.getPublic().getEncoded();
```

```
System.out.println("Sending Encoded Public Key- " +
            bobPubKeyEnc.length + " bytes");
ByteBuffer encodedCert = ByteBuffer.wrap(bobPubKeyEnc);
sent = sc.write(encodedCert);
```

```
        System.out.println("Execute PHASE1 ...");
```

```
B5      BobKeyAgree.doPhase(alicePubKey, true);
        byte[] bobSharedSecret = bobKeyAgree.generateSecret();
```

```
        System.out.println("Shared secret (DEBUG ONLY): " +
                    CryptoUtil.toHexString(bobSharedSecret));
```

```
B6      BobKeyAgree.doPhase(alicePubKey, true);
        SecretKey bobDesKey = bobKeyAgree.generateSecret("DES");
```

```
        byte[] recoveredPlaintext = CryptoUtil.readFromSocketChannel(sc);
        Cipher bobCipher = Cipher.getInstance("DES/ECB/PKCS5Padding");
        bobCipher.init(Cipher.DECRYPT_MODE, bobDesKey);
        String recovered = new String(bobCipher.doFinal(recoveredPlaintext));
        System.out.println("Decrypted Message: " + recovered);

        bobCipher.init(Cipher.ENCRYPT_MODE, bobDesKey);
        byte[] plaintext = "Beat Michigan!".getBytes("UTF-8");
        byte[] ciphertext = bobCipher.doFinal(plaintext);

        System.out.println("Sending encrypted response");
        ByteBuffer cipherBuf = ByteBuffer.wrap(ciphertext);
        sent = sc.write(cipherBuf);

        response = new String(CryptoUtil.readFromSocketChannel(sc));
        System.out.print("Received: " + response);

    } catch (NoSuchAlgorithmException e)
    {
        e.printStackTrace();
    } catch (InvalidKeySpecException e)
```

```
        {
            e.printStackTrace();
        } catch (InvalidAlgorithmParameterException e)
        {
            e.printStackTrace();
        } catch (InvalidKeyException e)
        {
            e.printStackTrace();
        } catch (NoSuchPaddingException e)
        {
            e.printStackTrace();
        } catch (IllegalStateException e)
        {
            e.printStackTrace();
        } catch (IllegalBlockSizeException e)
        {
            e.printStackTrace();
        } catch (BadPaddingException e)
        {
            e.printStackTrace();
        } finally
        {
            // Make sure we close the channel (and hence the socket)
            if (sc != null) sc.close();
        }
} catch (IOException ioe)
{
    ioe.printStackTrace();
}
```

After Bob's server acknowledges the *Hello* handshake from Alice, Alice sends over her encoded public key. In **B1**, we retrieve Alice's encoded public key off of the wire. In **B2,** we create an instance of a KeyFactory, first used by the LoadPublicKey example earlier in this chapter. The KeyFactory is used here to convert our encoded byte[] into an instance of a PublicKey. We do this by wrapping the encoded byte[] inside of an X509EncodedKeySpec. Once we have an instance of Alice's public key, we cast it to a DHPublicKey and extract out the parameters used in the generation of that *public* key, obtaining a DHParameterSpec. Realize that by itself, there isn't enough information inside of the public key to resolve the physical private key.

In **B3**, we create Bob's DH KeyPairGenerator instance, initializing it using the transparent parameters stored in the DHParameterSpec instance we extracted from Alice's public key. This establishes a common thread between Alice's public key and Bob's key generation that is about to take place. Bob obtains his KeyPair instance at the end of **B3**.

In **B4**, Bob obtains a DH KeyAgreement instance. Similar to where we left off with Alice's client, he too initializes the KeyAgreement instance using his private key. Recall that Alice is waiting to receive Bob's DH public key. We extract Bob's encoded public key and transmit that back over to Alice, where she receives it in **A4**.

Bob and Alice now have all of the information needed to successfully generate a shared secret key between them. Let's look at Bob's actions first. In **B5**, the doPhase() method on the KeyAgreement instance is invoked, passing in Alice's public key. The true indicates that this is the last phase of the key agreement. With the first (and last) phase of DH complete, we can now invoke the generateSecret() method and extract a byte[] that is the shared secret key. Similar to the way the Cipher engine works when its doFinal() method is invoked, the KeyAgreement instance is reset after the invocation of the generateSecret() method. Since the code example prints out the shared secret on the screen for debug and comparison with what Alice generated, the KeyAgreeement instance has been reset. We therefore reinvoke doPhase() in **B6** and obtain a DES SecretKey from the KeyAgreement instance that we use in the symmetric cipher that follows in the code. If the code hadn't dumped out the secret key so that we could compare what Bob generated to that which Alice generated, we only would have invoked doPhase() once.

Back in **A5** Alice goes through the motions to turn the encoded public key byte[] into a PublicKey instance. Once she has Bob's public key in hand, in **A6** she invokes the doPhase() method on her KeyAgreement instance. We see a similar situation here where for debug and comparison purposes we dump the shared secret that Alice generates out to the screen, forcing us to invoke doPhase() a second time. Realistically, this second invocation isn't necessary.

Let's compare the secrets that Bob and Alice generated. In Figures 3.1 and 3.2, we can see that Alice and Bob reached the same secret key—1D:04:8F:36 ... AB:49. They were able to reach this shared secret by only exposing DH public key instances to one another. And now that Alice and Bob have a common shared secret in the form of a SecretKey instance between them, they are free to proceed with their conversation using a symmetric cipher, knowing that it's encrypted and protected from prying eyes. In this example, we are using DES as the symmetric cipher, but we could have requested virtually any other supported

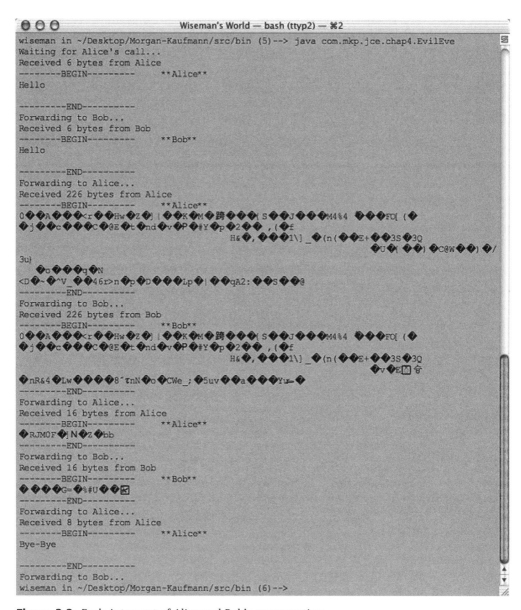

Figure 3.3: Eve's intercept of Alice and Bob's conversation.

cipher algorithm. For a refresher on the actual Cipher engine operation in the code examples, flip back to Chapter 2. Now let's look at Eve's intercept of the conversation between Alice and Bob. Eve's intercept of the conversation between Alice and Bob is pictured in Figure 3.3.

The code found in com.mkp.jce.chap3.EvilEve doesn't contain any cryptographic operations. In fact, it's merely a listen and rebroadcast engine that writes the intercepted output to the screen. For that reason, we aren't going to print the EvilEve code here and just review the screen shot. Of particular interest is that we can see the protocol in clear text, so Eve knows that she has successfully intercepted the conversation between Alice and Bob. Notice the exchanges that were 226 bytes in length. These were the DH public keys being exchanged. Even though Eve has intercepted these public keys, she lacks the private key data to successfully create a KeyAgreement instance of her own to extract the shared secret. The only thing Eve can do is hopelessly watch as Alice and Bob enter encrypted communications. Where Figures 3.1 and 3.2 show the plaintext messages that Alice and Bob exchanged, properly deciphered, Eve can only see the ciphertext as it passes by.

## chapter 4

Message Digests, Message Authentication Codes, and Digital Signatures

Message digests, message authentication codes, and digital signatures are all based on a notion of **hashing**. Hashing is one of those 50-cent words that simply means *convert*. Actually, according to the on-line version of the *Merriam-Webster Dictionary*, hashing means "to chop (as meat and potatoes) into small pieces." In our case, replace the *meat and potatoes* with *data*. We want to chop or convert a large piece of data into a smaller, more manageable piece of data that we can easily work with in memory. In cryptographic terms, another key characteristic we demand from a hash function is a fixed-length hash value, regardless if the input data is 1K or 10,000K in size. Knowing the size of the hash produced upfront is especially advantageous because Java is a strongly typed language. Unlike symmetric and asymmetric ciphers, hashing does not require the use of a key.

Cryptographic hashing requires the use of a **one-way hash function**. The best analogy I've heard for this property came from Bruce Schneier: he described a one-way hash as being similar to breaking a plate [26]. To expand on the analogy, anyone can smash a plate into a million pieces; however, taking all of those pieces and rebuilding the plate is unrealistic.

An important property of the one-way hash function is that it must be *collision-free*. Simply stated, no two disparate images should result in the same hash value. If only a single-bit changes, we should receive a *radically* different hash value from the underlying one-way hash function. Through this property, we have a means of validating the integrity of the original data. Let's say that I generate a hash out of a given document and store that value. Later on, if I need to validate that the document didn't change by even a single bit, I can rerun the document through the same one-way hash function. If the identical one-way hash function is used both times and the resulting hash values match, I'm reasonably assured that the document didn't change—not even by a single bit.

The strength of a one-way hash lies in the underlying hash function itself. To clarify, neither the hash value nor the one-way hash function is treated as secret. The mathematical properties of the hash function represent the true value, ensuring that no two disparate documents result in identical hash values.

This chapter looks at the natural progression from generating message digests, to combining the one-way hash function of the message digest with a key pair for authentication purposes, and it ultimately defines the role and use of digital signatures.

> Note: Each code sample in this chapter uses the same file so that you can compare the output of the different operations. This sample log file is from the Apache Jakarta Velocity project that was running on my machine. This file can be found inside of the `com.mkp.jce.chap4` package directory. Be sure to copy this file into your working directory, or alternatively update the code to reflect an accurate absolute path before running any of the examples.

4.1   Choosing a Message Digest Algorithm

A **Message Digest** is the more commonly used term used to represent a one-way hash function, and the hash value result is simply referred to as the *digest*. In many ways, by distancing themselves from the term "hash," people are less likely to encounter confusion between a cryptographic hash (i.e., one-way hash) and a hash used in an intrinsic data structure like the `java.util.Hashtable` class, which is unsuitable for use in cryptographic operations. The term "Message Digest" originally stems from the one-way hash functions *MD2, MD4,* and *MD5*, where the MD stood for message digest. Each of these algorithms yields a 128-bit digest. MD2 was optimized for an 8-bit architecture, where MD4 and MD5 targeted 32-bit architectures. Needless to say, we will not be performing any MD2 calculations today.

Cryptographers and mathematicians (for no particular reason) have spent more time working to develop and analyze ciphers than they have message digests, random number generators, and the other aspects of cryptography. The message digest choices are small, with only three predominate algorithms.

4.1.1   An Overview of an MD5

MD5 is more secure than MD4 [20], and the `SunJCE` provider includes support for the MD5 algorithm. MD5 hashes are 128-bits in length. There are papers published [21] that describe a weakness in the underlying mechanics of the algorithm that could lead to collisions—a violation of the collision-free properties we expect for a cryptographic one-way hash. While there is no known documentation that describes how to exploit this information to attack the algorithm, knowing that the risk is there would suggest that it is prudent to avoid the use of MD5 where possible.

4.1.2 An Overview of SHA-1

The other predominate one-way hashing algorithm is the **Secure Hash Algorithm 1** function, or simply *SHA-1*. SHA-1 is an algorithm designed by the NSA [14,15], with every hashing operation resulting in a 20-byte (160-bit) hash, slightly larger than the 128-bit hash produced by an MD5 operation. In cryptography, every bit counts, literally, and the meager increase in hash size may result in a noticeably slower hash generation on large files compared with MD5. SHA-1 has been backed by NIST, and, in fact, NIST recently published three new derivations: SHA-256, SHA-384, and SHA-512. Earlier, we stated that message digests haven't been studied as extensively as ciphers, and these new algorithms epitomize that point. I would suggest waiting for the gurus to analyze these new methods further before coding to them unless you can cite specific reasons why SHA-1 doesn't meet your needs. For those who do venture into these new algorithms, there is little value in a SHA-384 because it requires a computational workload equivalent to an SHA-512, so grab the extra bits and use the SHA-512.

4.1.3 An Overview of RIPEMD

Originally developed for the European Community's RIPE project [23], this algorithm is similar in nature to the MD4 algorithm. The RIPEMD128 and RIPEMD160 produce message digests that are 128- and 160-bits in length, respectively. Many third party providers, including Bouncy Castle and Cryptix, provide RIPEMD implementations.

Now that we've covered the predominate message digests, let's look at how the MessageDigest engine is used.

4.2 **The** MessageDigest **Engine**

The JCA introduced an engine specific for working with cryptographic one-way hash functions, the MessageDigest engine. The SUN provider supports MD5 and SHA-1 natively, and other providers may offer their alternative message digest algorithms.

4.2.1 Code Example: Generating a Message Digest

Let's look at a message digest example in action. This example will read in a file and produce a message digest for it. We will use the MD5 message digest.

Example 4.1 Sample Code Location: com.mkp.jce.chap4.MessageDigestExample

```
1  StringBuffer buf = new StringBuffer();

2

3  try
```

```
4  {
5      //Be sure to copy the velocity.log to your working directory
6      //or change to an absolute path to ensure the files found
7      FileInputStream fis = new FileInputStream(
8              new File("./velocity.log"));
9
10     int curChar=0;
11     while( (curChar = fis.read()) != -1 )
12     {
13             buf.append((char) curChar);
14     }
15 } catch (IOException ioe)
16 {
17     //Handle this!
18     System.out.println("Couldn't find the file. Check the path!");
19     System.exit(0);
20 }
21
22 try
23 {
24     MessageDigest md5 = MessageDigest.getInstance("MD5");
25     md5.update(buf.toString().getBytes("UTF-8"));
26
27     byte[] digest = md5.digest();
28     System.out.println("MD5 Digest Length: " + digest.length);
29
30     for(int i =0;i<digest.length;i++)
31     {
32             System.out.print(digest[i] + " ");
33     }
```

```
34      System.out.println("");
35
36 } catch (NoSuchAlgorithmException nsae)
37 {
38      nsae.printStackTrace();
39 } catch (UnsupportedEncodingException use)
40      use.printStackTrace();
41 }
```

The first try...catch block is pure Java I/O to read in the file or message that we want to produce the digest from. Line 24 invokes the opaque factory method, requesting an instance for the highest priority provider that can supply an MD5 message digest implementation. The MessageDigest engine operates conceptually in an identical fashion to its cousin, the Cipher engine. Recall that the Cipher engine supports single-part or multipart operation. Multipart operations involved invoking the update() method 1...* times, and on the last slice of data invoking the doFinal() method. The doFinal() method wrapped up the cipher encryption operation, reset the engine preparing it for another encryption operation immediately, and returned the ciphertext as a byte[] to the calling routine. The MessageDigest engine also supports single-part and multipart operations. You can invoke the update() method 1...* times and on the last slice of data invoke the digest() method to gather the result. Alternatively, you can directly invoke the digest() method if they have all of the data available and get the result. With either approach, upon invocation of the digest() method, the engine wraps up the digest calculation, resets the engine preparing it for another digest calculation immediately, and returns the digest as a byte[] to the calling routine. On line 25, the sample invokes the update() method, passing in the byte[] from the velocity.log file, and then it invokes the digest() method with no arguments on line 27, collecting the result. An equivalent coding solution would have been to invoke the digest method directly, for example:

```
byte[] digest = md5.digest(buf.toString().getBytes("UTF-8"));
```

MD5 digest results are always 128-bits long (16 bytes). Execution of the sample against the velocity.log (assuming it hasn't been modified!) should yield a digest that reads:

```
MD5 Digest Length: 16
59 80 2 -116 35 1 -107 116 57 -117 -41 2 -86 -86 63 27
```

Now, let's show an experiment that demonstrates one of the qualities we desire in a cryptographic one-way hash. Previously, we stated that if a single-bit changes, we should receive a *radically* different digest from the underlying one-way hash function. In our case, we are going to change one character at the top of the log file. Originally, the third line of the log file read:

```
2003-06-13 18:27:13,191 - Starting Jakarta Velocity v1.3
```

We are going to simply capitalize the middle 'a' in Jakarta, so that the third line of the log now reads:

```
2003-06-13 18:27:13,191 - Starting JakArta Velocity v1.3
```

Now, we rerun our sample and compare the results.

```
MD5 Digest Length: 16

-35 77 20 16 -119 4 -109 -49 -72 59 -7 -107 -83 35 47 -85
```

Wow! Look at how radically different the values of the digest turn out with only a single character change. We could have chosen to use a SHA-1 digest as well by simply modifying the factory method request on line 24 and updating the System.out.println statement on line 28 to read SHA-1 instead of MD5. The larger SHA-1 digest from the *original* velocity.log file is radically different than the MD5 digest, yielding a 160-bit (20 byte) result and a different set of values:

```
SHA-1 Digest Length: 20

104 82 97 -102 116 -65 75 -61 107 27 108 -57 -112 -107 50 -39 20 -105 -40 114
```

4.2.2   Message Digest Performance

A lot of people talk about the cost of doing the cryptographic work inside of an application. Rest assured, *substantially* more time is spent animating the icons and drawing pretty shadows than on the security of any application out there. However, that doesn't dismiss the need for a benchmark on performance in cases where you require a high-speed, low-drag solution. The most rudimentary of tests were performed using venerable System.currentTimeMillis() calls. Here's what the sample code looked like (sans try...catch blocks).

```
MessageDigest md5 = MessageDigest.getInstance("digest algorithm here");


long start = System.currentTimeMillis();

byte[] digest = md5.digest(buf.toString().getBytes("UTF-8"));

long end = System.currentTimeMillis();


System.out.println("Duration: " + (end-start));
```

My test platform was a dual 1 GHz PowerPC G4 Mac with 1.25GB of RAM. When running with the MD5 digest algorithm from the SUN provider, the times ranged from 35 to 41 milliseconds. The SHA-1 digest resulted in substantially faster times (comparatively), ranging from 15 to 19 milliseconds. Things to consider include the size of the velocity.log file—it's relatively small compared with larger, real-world messages. Additionally, both tests endured music blaring from my iTunes application running in the background!

4.2.3   Understanding Message Digest Shortcomings

On the surface, it would appear that a message digest works great for ensuring that a message hasn't been tampered with. Our simple example of changing the case of a single letter resulted in a dramatically different digest. However, there is a serious flaw in using a message digest by itself when you are transmitting the document and the digest in real-time (e.g., e-mail or perhaps an FTP architecture). The problem is known as the "Man in the Middle" attack. In this scenario, Alice is sending Bob a very important legal document, and, along with the document, she is sending the message digest algorithm name that she used (SHA-1) and the resulting digest, all 20 bytes. When she sends the mail, Eve is lurking in the shadows and intercepts the network traffic before it leaves Alice's ISP. Eve modifies the document, generates a new SHA-1 digest, and replaces the attachments on the e-mail with the modified versions. Bob receives the document and the digest, verifies the document produces an identical SHA-1 digest, and assumes that the message is authentic. Bob just got duped! How do we overcome this situation? Well, to reiterate a previous point, message digests neither operate with a secret key, nor are they intended to be kept secret. There is nothing sensitive inside of the document that demands the use of encryption; it's a simple limited Power of Attorney document (for example). Beyond that, there is a subtle but even more important point. Encryption works to prevent someone from reading a message, not from tampering with it. If the cipher used Electronic Code Book (ECB) for the cipher mode, then blocks of the message could be shifted around or replaced without any way of proving the modifications took place. (And that's why the use of other *chaining* cipher modes is highly recommended!) So how do Alice and Bob ensure that the document arrives in Bob's hands in its original form, authenticated that it came directly from Alice without modification through a "Man in the Middle" attack? Enter the message authentication code (MAC)!

4.3   **The Mac Engine**

As we've just seen, sometimes generating a digest isn't secure enough, especially when the document and the digest could be intercepted before they reach their intended recipient. A **MAC** combines the use of a message digest with a secret key known only to Alice and Bob. Instead of producing only a digest of the submitted bytes, the submitted bytes are combined with the secret key to generate the digest. What is gained through the addition of the secret key? Well, only the individual with the secret key has the ability to validate the digest. Beyond the addition of the secret key, the properties and characteristics of the MAC are for all intensive purposes identical to a message digest. In fact, conceptually, by publishing the secret key that was used, the MAC is effectively turned into a vanilla message digest.

4.3.1 Code Example: Generating a Hashed MAC Digest

Before the calculation of the digest, the engine *must* be initialized. Initialization is completed once the secret key has been provided to the engine. Any javax.crypto.SecretKey instance will suffice. This robust design means that the SecretKey could originate from either a KeyGenerator (covered in-depth in Chapter 2) or from a KeyAgreement operation (covered in-depth in Chapter 3). Using the SecretKey, invoke the init() method.

Once the SecretKey is obtained and the Mac engine initialization is complete, the engine is ready to go to work. The Mac engine supports either a single-part or multipart operation. Since this engine was introduced as part of the JCE, it uses the same nomenclature as the Cipher engine. In a single-part operation, a single invocation of the doFinal() method is required. Multipart operations invoke the update() method 1...* times, and conclude with a call to the doFinal() method. In either approach, the invocation of the doFinal() method concludes the operation and resets the engine.

Example 4.2 Sample Code Location: com.mkp.jce.chap4.MacExample

```
//NOTE: The buf is populated using an identical try...catch block

//from the MessageDigestExample and reads the same velocity.log file


1    try

2    {

3        //Get an HMac SHA-1 Key Generator

4        KeyGenerator kg = KeyGenerator.getInstance("HMACMD5");

5

6        //Generate the SecretKey

7        SecretKey key = kg.generateKey();

8

9        //Get an HMac SHA-1 instance

10       Mac mac = Mac.getInstance("hmacmd5");

11

12       //Initialize the Mac with the secret key
```

```
13      //Some providers may require a special
14      //secret key (check provider docs), in
15      //which case an inadequate key throws
16      //an InvalidKeyException
17      mac.init(key);
18
19      byte[] digest = mac.doFinal(buf.toString().getBytes("UTF-8"));
20
21      System.out.println("HMac MD5 Digest Length: " + digest.length);
22
23      for(int i=0;i<digest.length;i++)
24      {
25              System.out.print(digest[i] + " ");
26      }
27      System.out.println("");
28
29 } catch (NoSuchAlgorithmException nsae)
30 {
31      nsae.printStackTrace();
32 } catch (InvalidKeyException ike)
33 {
34      ike.printStackTrace();
35 } catch (UnsupportedEncodingException use)
36      use.printStackTrace();
37 }
```

This sample uses the same velocity.log file used in the MessageDigestExample (the try...catch block used to perform the Java I/O has been cropped in the interest of space). For continuity, this example is also based on the MD5 message digest. Lines 4 and 10 request an opaque HMacMD5 implementation. The acronym HMAC stands for *hashing message authentication code* alluding to the fact that a one-way hashing algorithm is being used to generate the MAC. The SunJCE provider supports both MD5 and SHA-1 HMAC implementations under the names HMACMD5 and HMACSHA1, respectively. As discussed in Chapter 1, all engine algorithm parameters are case-*insensitive*. On line 4 we obtain a KeyGenerator that is capable of producing a secret key for an HMACMD5 implementation, invoking generateKey() on line 7. The SunJCE provider has no expectations about the key passed into the init() method on line 17. However, other providers may be more particular about the MAC key—consult your provider's documentation for details. If the provider doesn't approve of the key, rest assured you'll see an InvalidKeyException thrown! Let's look at the output of the sample:

```
HMac MD5 Digest Length: 16

-83 123 -33 -11 123 2 12 -88 94 87 73 -57 6 98 -25 85
```

The resulting digest is still 128-bits in length, but it is different from the vanilla MD5 message digest because of the addition of the secret key. This effectively counters the *Man in the Middle* attack in broadcast situations. Alice now sends Bob the message and the digest, and because only Alice and Bob know the secret key, Eve can still intercept the message, but she's lost her ability to tamper with the contents and forward a modified message to Bob.

Another popular approach for generating the secret key is to directly employ a CSPRNG, avoiding the opaque KeyGenerator approach (most leverage a similar CSPRNG approach, so there is no real advantage to coding it one way or the other). For example, replace lines 4 through 7 with the following code block:

```
SecureRandom csprng = SecureRandom.getInstance("SHA1PRNG");

byte[] randomBytes = new byte[16];

csprng.nextBytes(randomBytes);

SecretKeySpec key = new SecretKeySpec(randomBytes, "HMACMD5");
```

Regardless of which approach you use, you are responsible for actually saving out the secret key. In Chapter 5, we'll investigate the KeyStore engine and how it can be used to store secret keys. In cases where a MAC is used for personal reassurance (you generate a MAC for a set of files on hard drive to ensure no one modifies those files without your knowledge), a good KeyStore implementation solution is more than adequate. However, in cases where you are going to be transmitting the data, you should consider using a KeyAgreement engine to automatically handle key management on both sides of the conversation. (This is a much better solution than trying to devise your own protocol that would allow Alice to share the secret key with Bob.)

4.3.2 Understanding MAC Shortcomings

Employing a MAC provides reasonable assurances that the content of a message hasn't been tampered with. However, by itself it is not a panacea for every type of attack that could take place on a message. For example, Eve could still intercept the message and the digest and rebroadcast it to Bob months later, perhaps contradicting previous messages from Alice and successfully introducing confusion, since Bob was able to authenticate the message using his copy of the secret key. To overcome this in situations where a regular conversation takes place, consider incorporating some type of timestamp. As the timestamp changes, so does the digest. When Bob receives a message with a timestamp out of sequence, he merely discards the message as a fraud because Alice could not have sent it. Eve can attempt to modify the timestamp, but doing so invalidates the digest, and Bob will again know it is a fraud.

But what if the timestamp was part of the protocol and not included in the computation of the MAC? This design flaw could be exploited by Eve, and her replay attack could work. The Horton Principle [22] tells us to authenticate what is being *meant*, not what is being said. Ensure that the MAC covers the meaning of the message and not just the raw data. Overlooking the little things, like the timestamp, can result in an exploitable security lapse.

4.4 Digital Signatures

Digital signatures are intended to provide similar characteristics to those of handwritten signatures. In fact, the most important aspect of a digital signature is that in certain countries, under certain situations, it carries the same weight in a court of law as a handwritten signature. Signing a physical piece of paper with a handwritten signature or signing a purchase order with a digital signature both carry equal weight thanks to laws passed in the United States during the Clinton administration's second term. Those with a corollary interest in digital law should take a look at the Digital Signature Law Survey by Simone van der Hof at http://rechten.uvt.nl/simone/ds-lawsu.htm.

Let's revisit our nonrepudiation example from Chapter 2, section 2.5.2. Alice and Bob decide to use a symmetric cipher to exchange purchase orders, invoices, and shipping manifests between each of their companies, but they have the foresight to realize that they need an intermediary to pull this off. They identify a common company TrustMe, Inc. that they both know and trust. Instead of Alice sending her orders directly to Bob, she forwards them using a secret key shared only between her and TrustMe, Inc. There, TrustMe, Inc. decrypts Alice's message, adds a statement validating that Alice is truly placing this order, and encrypts the message using a secret key shared only between TrustMe, Inc. and Bob. Despite the addition of the trusted third party, has anything really changed? No, not really. TrustMe, Inc. doesn't have any better tools available to verify the order came from Alice than when the message went straight from Alice to Bob. Beyond that, there is now an additional step in the process that serves as a potential bottleneck in the system. A better solution is still needed, and it must offer true nonrepudiation capabilities and not pose a bottleneck in the business process.

The solution to providing a digital signature lies in the application of public and private keys. If Alice digitally signs her purchase order with her private key—a key that is never shared with anyone, and Bob is able to successfully decrypt the purchase order signature using Alice's public key, then the purchase order must be from Alice's private key. This clearly provides a form of nonrepudiation. Nothing in the purchase order document is considered confidential, and Alice and Bob agree there is no need to encrypt the contents of the document; the document merely needs to be signed. The application of a message digest can help solve this problem. Let's let Alice run through the motions again using this new technique that involves a message digest combined with an asymmetric cipher.

1. Alice generates her purchase order for Bob and generates a digest of the document using a SHA-1 one-way hash function.

2. Alice then uses her private key to encrypt the digest—all 160-bits of the digest. The purchase order stays in plaintext form, and the encrypted digest is sent alongside the purchase order with a statement in plaintext that a SHA-1 one-way hash was used to compute the digest.

3. Bob receives the purchase order in its plain text form as well as the indication that a SHA-1 one-way hash function was used to produce the digest.

4. Bob runs the purchase order through an implementation of the SHA-1 one-way hash function and computes the 160-bit digest.

5. Using Alice's public key, Bob decrypts the digest Alice sent along with the purchase order. He then compares his digest to the decrypted digest he obtained with the message. If the digests match, then Bob knows that

   a. The document hasn't been tampered with

   b. Only Alice's private key could have been used to sign the digest

The JCA includes an implementation of the **digital signature algorithm** (DSA), which provides all of the mechanisms necessary to accomplish this overall signature process without so many steps. Much to the disquietude of RSA, which had long been regarded as the de facto public key implementation, in May 1994 the U.S. Government, via the National Institute of Standards and Technology (NIST) and the National Security Agency (NSA), established the Digital Signature Standard (DSS). The DSS uses the DSA as its cornerstone algorithm for generating signatures. Unlike the more powerful (and widely used) RSA algorithms, the DSA is not suitable for use in an encryption operation and is intended only for use in a digital signature scheme. Beyond this fact, let's look at the speed characteristics of the two. Looking only at RSA, the generation of an RSA signature is slow, and the verification of an RSA signature is extremely fast (comparatively). To the contrary, the DSA is fast in signature generation and slow in verification [24]. However, since the introduction of these algorithms, processor speeds have increased dramatically, and in many situations the speed difference is negligible to human perception. If you are inquiring which signature standard should be used, the RSA is the logical choice. It has been around longer, and ideally you only sign a document once and verify it many times, which its speed characteristics are well tailored toward. Hence, all of the examples that follow revolve around the RSA algorithms.

4.5 The Signature Engine

The JCA supports digital signatures through the Signature engine. Both sides use this engine—the person generating the signature first and later the person verifying the signature. It operates similar to the Cipher engine in that it must be initialized to do one or the other but never both at the same time. Let's jump right into a code example showing how to generate a digital signature.

4.5.1 Code Example: Generating a Digital Signature Using a Private Key

This code example demonstrates how to generate a signature only. We will use the RSA key pair generated from the code sample GenerateKeyPair found in Chapter 3 and assume 'jcebook' was used as the base name, giving us two files named /jcebook.pubkey and /jcebook.privkey. We'll use the same velocity.log file used in the previous digest examples.

Example 4.3 Sample Code Location: com.mkp.jce.chap4.ApplySignature

```
1   try
2   {
3       String fileData =
4               CryptoUtil.readPlainTextFile(new File("/velocity.log"));
5
6       FileInputStream fis = new FileInputStream(new File("/jcebook.privkey"));
7
8       ByteArrayOutputStream privKeyBaos = new ByteArrayOutputStream();
9
10      int curByte=0;
11      while( (curByte = fis.read()) != -1 )
12      {
13              privKeyBaos.write(curByte);
14      }
15
16      PKCS8EncodedKeySpec keySpec =
17              new PKCS8EncodedKeySpec(privKeyBaos.toByteArray());
18      privKeyBaos.close();
```

```
19
20      KeyFactory keyFactoryEngine = KeyFactory.getInstance("RSA");
21      PrivateKey privateKey = keyFactoryEngine.generatePrivate(keySpec);
22
23      Signature signatureEngine = Signature.getInstance("MD5withRSA");
24
25      //Initialize the signature to be in sign mode
26      signatureEngine.initSign(privateKey);
27
28      //Pass in the bytes of our velocity.log sample file
29      signatureEngine.update(fileData.getBytes("UTF-8"));
30
31      //Obtain the signature
32      byte[] signature = signatureEngine.sign();
33
34      //Save the signature for use in the VerifySignature code sample
35      FileOutputStream fos = new FileOutputStream(new File("/signature.data"));
36      fos.write(signature);
37      fos.close();
38
39      System.out.println("MD5 with RSA Signature Length: " + signature.length);
40      for(int i =0;i < signature.length;i++)
41      {
42              System.out.print(signature[i] + " ");
43      }
44      System.out.println("");
45
46 } catch (IOException ioe)
47 {
48      ioe.printStackTrace();
```

```
49 } catch (NoSuchAlgorithmException nsae)

50 {

51    nsae.printStackTrace();

52 } catch (InvalidKeySpecException ikse)

53 {

54    ikse.printStackTrace();

55 } catch (InvalidKeyException ike)

56 {

57    ike.printStackTrace();

58 } catch (SignatureException se)

59 {

60    se.printStackTrace();

61 }
```

We load the file that we want to sign in lines 3–4, and our private key's encoded bytes over lines 8–14. Knowing that private keys are stored using PKCS#8 encoding, lines 16 through 21 process the encoded bytes and yield a PrivateKey instance that will be used to generate the signature. On line 23 we request an instance of an MD5withRSA signature engine and initialize the engine for a signature operation on line 26, passing in our RSA private key. We invoke the update() method on the signature instance on line 29 and request the final signature on line 32. We then write out the signature on lines 35–37 to a file named "signature.data" for future reference.

One important thing to realize is that despite the nomenclature used, "signing" a document really doesn't modify the document in any way. In fact, we generate an additional document (one that isn't really legible unless you like reading bytes). If Alice wanted to send her co-worker Bob a signed document in an e-mail, she would include two attachments: the original unmodified document and the signature.data file. Alice and Bob previously exchanged public keys. Along with these two files, she informs Bob that an MD5withRSA signature was generated. Let's see what Bob has to do when he receives Alice's e-mail.

4.5.2   Code Example: Verifying a Digital Signature Using a Public Key

Bob receives both attachments and sets out to ensure that the original document wasn't tampered with during transport. To do so, Bob uses the Signature engine, but this time it will be operated in verify mode. The engine will compare the signature it generates from the file Alice sent Bob to the signature Alice provided.

Example 4.4 Sample Code Location: com.mkp.jce.chap4.VerifySignature

```
1   try
2   {
3       String fileData =
4               CryptoUtil.readPlainTextFile(new File("/velocity.log"));
5
6       PublicKey publicKey =
7               CryptoUtil.loadPublicKey(new File("/jcebook.pubkey"), "RSA");
8
9       byte[] signatureFromAlice =
10              CryptoUtil.readSignatureFile(new File("/signature.data"));
11      Signature signatureEngine = Signature.getInstance("MD5withRSA");
12
13      //Initialize the signature to be in verify mode
14      signatureEngine.initVerify(publicKey);
15
16      //Pass in the bytes of our velocity.log sample file
17      signatureEngine.update(fileData.getBytes("UTF-8"));
18
19
20      boolean isVerified = false;
21      try
22      {
23              isVerified = signatureEngine.verify(signatureFromAlice);
24      } catch (SignatureException se)
25      {
26              //you could report the problem here!
27              System.out.println("Uh-oh. Looks like trouble!");
```

```
28    }

29    System.out.println("Verified: " + isVerified);

30

31 } catch (IOException ioe)

32 {

33    ioe.printStackTrace();

34 } catch (NoSuchAlgorithmException nsae)

35 {

36    nsae.printStackTrace();

37 } catch (InvalidKeySpecException ikse)

38 {

39    ikse.printStackTrace();

40 } catch (InvalidKeyException ike)

41 {

42    ike.printStackTrace();

43 } catch (SignatureException se)

44 {

45    se

46 }
```

Lines 3–10 load the three files required to validate a document and signature reportedly from Alice: the message itself, Alice's RSA public key, and the signature data Alice generated using her RSA private key. With this information available, Bob requests a Signature engine of the same type Alice used (conveyed in Alice's e-mail body) on line 11 and initializes it on line 14 for verification using Alice's public key. He passes in the bytes of the file that needs verified on line 17, and on line 23 invokes the verify() method passing in the signature data from Alice (generated with Alice's private key). If the output indicates the signature is valid, Bob can now form two very strong conclusions about the file:

1. The message hasn't been tampered with—not a single bit changed since Alice's private key created the signature

2. Alice's private key was used to generate the signature, and any repudiation argument from Alice would be difficult.

For all intents and purposes, Bob has authenticated that Alice was involved and knows about the content of the document, but its important to understand that if some-one obtained a copy of Alice's private RSA key, then it is possible the document is forged.

## chapter 5

Managing Keys and Certificates

This chapter formally introduces digital certificates and discusses several key management strategies for certificates and symmetric cipher keys. Digital certificates represent a core part of a commonly discussed, rarely achieved public key infrastructure (PKI). Even if your organization hasn't implemented a PKI solution, there will still be times when digital certificates may be useful. We'll look at how we can use the keytool utility to generate some DSA certificates suitable for signing and some RSA certificates suitable for either signing or encryption. Once we have a couple sample certificates, we'll walk through several code examples that include reading and storing certificates encoded using basic encoding rules (BER), distinguished encoding rules (DER), and Base64. We'll also briefly review an encryption example where we use the public key from an RSA certificate to initialize the Cipher engine.

Tracking and managing secret keys, key pairs, and digital certificates can be a major undertaking in some situations. This chapter also introduces Java's key store, an interface for managing large collections of these items. Since we'll want a place to store our digital certificates, we start by discussing key management needs and the Java key store.

5.1 The Need for Key Management

Of all things mathematicians can solve, key management isn't one of them. Ultimately, the custody chain involves people, and the fact is people are neither perfect nor machines. People lose their car keys, that letter from Aunt May, and yes, that file that contained their key.

Cryptography can be a two-edged sword. By that I mean that as much as it helps, it has the potential to hurt. For example, if you encrypt that secret message, and then you lose the key that you used to encrypt it, that message may be irretrievable. The same algorithms that were intended to keep prying eyes from reading your memos are now keeping you from reading your memos. In fact, the situation could be even worse—imagine losing your key and it finds its way into the hands of irreparable individuals; suddenly those secret memos are posted on the Internet for *everyone* to read. What does this all mean? Well, regardless of all of the mathematical proofs and empirical evidence that says your data will be most secure using Cipher X, the fact is, if your key is lost or, even worse, compromised, Cipher X has hurt you more than it helped you.

Here's another reality-based story that demonstrates the limits of cryptography, and while it isn't directly related to key management, it provides important insight into the limits of cryptography. There is a company that produces operating systems that also decided to dabble in the multi-media arena. They developed an extremely powerful media player that had what they marketed as "the most secure and robust set of digital rights management routines" (read cryptography) that industry had seen. It took hackers only a couple of hours after the product release to successfully intercept the digital media. You see, ultimately, the encrypted music files had to be deciphered and sent to the sound card to be played on the speakers. The hackers wrote a simple routine that sampled the sound card—the hardware—for the music as it passed through it, recording every bit. The net-net was that no matter how strong the key that encrypted the media was, or even how sophisticated the cipher was, the hackers intercepted the music with very little resistance.

In both of these examples, cryptography didn't fail. The cipher didn't lose its key, and the cipher has no control over the sound card's low-level APIs. It was either the people involved or outside factors in both equations that resulted in the loss of data. As we explore in this chapter the JCE's key management routines, I implore you to pay special attention to the outside factors, that is, things that a cipher can't control for you. The weakness in your security may have nothing to do with the size of the key being used.

5.2   Digital Certificates Defined

In isolation, a public key provides no real data about the person who or entity that holds the corresponding private key. The introduction of name-value fields in addition to a public key comprises a *digital certificate.* Now, there is tangible, value-added information along with the public key. Of course we quickly stumble on the next problem, and that is what stops someone from putting their name de jour and other bogus data in those fields? My digital certificate could state my name is King Arthur or Peter Pan or Brutus Buckeye. The digital certificate only takes on true meaning when a trusted third party, like VeriSign or Thawte, takes actions to validate the data in the certificate's fields, signing the certificate (digital signature) using their CA private key once a certain level of proof has been provided that the values in the certificate's fields are accurate. In this example, VeriSign or Thawte would be considered the *certificate authority* (CA), and once their digital signature is applied to my digital certificate, presumably you and everyone else will treat my certificate as a *trusted certificate.*

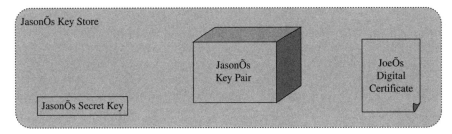

Figure 5.1: A key store holds secret keys, key pairs, and digital certificates.

In a PKI utopian society, there would be one and only one CA. In the real world, who would you trust to fulfill that role? An NYSE listed public company? The NSA? Microsoft? Hence the demise of the notion of PKI, as there is no suitable candidate to be that one CA. In fact, many organizations have strong desires (and often good reasons from their perspective) to become their own CA. We've already established that a trusted certificate is one that is digitally signed by the CA's private key, thereby verifiable on demand by the CA's own public digital certificate or root certificate. There are commercial offerings that will help deliver this vision to a company, and I'm not going to plug any of them here. Always weigh carefully material you read about PKI – how much of it is part of that unrealistic utopian dream and how much of it is tangible, usable material for the world in which we live.

5.3 The KeyStore Engine

The JCA defines the java.security.KeyStore engine class to manage secret keys, key pairs, and digital certificates. As an engine, it implements the standard pair of engine factory methods, for example:

```
KeyStore store = KeyStore.getInstance("JKS");
```

The KeyStore represents an *in-memory* representation of the keys it's protecting, as depicted in Figure 5.1. Each artifact placed in the key store is given an alias to easily identify it. This makes sense; running data through a Cipher didn't automatically write the cipher text out to a file somewhere; that was your responsibility.

After obtaining an instance of a KeyStore that can manage keys using the format you specified, you either point the instance to an InputStream that contains the keys to load into memory, or you use a null InputStream reference, implying that you want to create a new in-memory store. The in-memory reference also means that any state changes in the key store, that is, if you add or remove keys or certificates, are not immediately reflected to the original file until the store() method is invoked, passing an appropriate OutputStream as an argument.

There are in fact two key store formats available. The first and older format is from the JCA's SUN provider. It supports the "JKS" format, for *Java Key Store.* The second format is a newer keystore implementation included with the JCE's SunJCE provider. This newer format implements a much stronger (relatively speaking) protection of keys through the use of a PBE with Triple-DES algorithm. The java.security file defines JKS as the default key store type with its entry that reads keystore.type=jks in the middle of the file. Like all engine algorithm parameters, keystore types are case-insensitive, so you can refer to these stores programmatically as jks, JKS, JCEKS or jCeKs all with equal results. Unlike cipher algorithm parameters and keys that can be converted to a vendor-neutral format, KeyStore implementations are always considered proprietary, and thus never interchangeable.

The java.security.Security class offers a set of methods to dynamically read and modify (depending on the java.policy file's configuration in the JRE) properties from the java.security file. For example, the following line of code could be used by a utility application to read the user's preferred type of key store format. The resulting string is then passed into the KeyStore factory method, ensuring that the tool can use different formats without recompilation.

```
String defaultKeyStoreFormat = Security.getProperty("keystore.type");

KeyStore keyStore = KeyStore.getInstance(defaultKeyStoreFormat);
```

This technique is commonly used by the existing JCA utilities, including the keytool, jarsigner, and policytool. In fact, this technique is so common, there is a static method on the KeyStore class itself named getDefaultType() that saves you from having to import the Security class. This means that you could change your default key store format to say "BKS," which is one of the formats offered by the Bouncy Castle provider, and continue to use any of these tools as you did before. They would automatically use the new format.

Why all this fuss about key store formats? Each format has its own pros and cons. For example, the BKS key store format cited previously is tamper resistant but not encrypted (meaning that anyone could use an editor to inspect its contents). Other key store formats supported by the Bouncy Castle provider include Keystore.BouncyCastle (aliased as Keystore.UBER) and PKCS12. The former encrypts the entire key store using the Bouncy Castle PBEWithSHAAndTwofish-CBC algorithm, ensuring the entire key store is inspection- and tamper-resistant.

Of course, as many people have pointed out over the years, the command line doesn't suddenly stop printing plain text as soon as you hit the password argument, so anyone looking over your shoulder or who pulls up your command history can retrieve the password. In fact, this is another example of where people, not cryptography, break the equation. If you do command line key store work using the keytool or other utilities, it would be wise to close that shell window once you're done to eliminate the history attack by a passer-by! Another reason to consider key store format is because it surrounds the persistence mechanism being employed by the provider. Is the data going to be an in-memory representation only, sent to a file on your hard drive, be streamed via a serial port into a hardware device like a smart card, or perhaps sent across the network for storage in some LDAP server somewhere? The JCA doesn't enforce either a persistence require-ment or a persistence mechanism, leaving the provider a wide array of implementation choices.

Example 5.1 Sample Code Location: com.mkp.jce.chap5.CreateNewKeystore

```
1   try
2   {
3           //Using the factory method, load a keystore based
4           //on the user's java.security preferences
5           //Notice the getDefaultType() call to reflect user's prefs
6           KeyStore store = KeyStore.getInstance(KeyStore.getDefaultType());
7
8           //Before the KeyStore can be used, it has to be loaded.
9           //In this example, we pass null to indicate we want to
10          //create a new KeyStore for use, and no password since
11          //nothing needs validated
12          store.load(null, "".toCharArray());
13
14          //Open up an output stream to the new keystore's location
15          FileOutputStream fos = new FileOutputStream(
16                  new File("/jcebook.keystore"));
17
18          //Probably would prompt the user for this value
19          char[] password = new char[] {'s','e','c','r','e','t','c','o','d','e'};
20
21          //Write the keystore out to the file system.
22          store.store(fos, password);
23
24          //Clear the memory of the array's values
25          Arrays.fill(password, '\u0000');
26
```

```
27        System.out.println("Empty keystore created successfully!");

28

29 } catch(KeyStoreException kse)

30 {

31      kse.printStackTrace();

32 } catch (CertificateException ce)

33 {

34      ce.printStackTrace();

35 } catch (IOException ioe)

36 {

37      ioe.printStackTrace();

38 } catch (NoSuchAlgorithmException nse)

39 {

40      nse.printStackTrace();

41 }
```

Line 6 uses the strongly recommended technique of requesting a KeyStore engine based on the java.security preferences of the user's JVM, looking up the default keys store type. With this engine loaded, we pass a null InputStream reference into the load() method on line 12. Since the key store doesn't physically exist, there is no need during creation to provide a password to validate against the key store when using the JKS format. For other providers like the JCEKS or the Bouncy Castle implementations that put a type of PBE in front of the key store contents, the char array is the physical password that must be provided to even access the contents, presumably even the first time during key store creation. We open up a FileStream and save our empty key store to the indicated path in lines 15 through 25, making sure we clear out the in-memory representation of the password once we're done.

5.3.1   The **keytool** Utility

J2SE includes this nifty utility to work with key stores and to create certificates. Before we can continue with more code examples, we need to create some digital certificates using this utility. Rarely is there a need to dynamically create digital certificates on the fly from within software. Dynamically created certificates wouldn't be considered trusted certificates and are thus relegated to junk status in the real world. Production environments

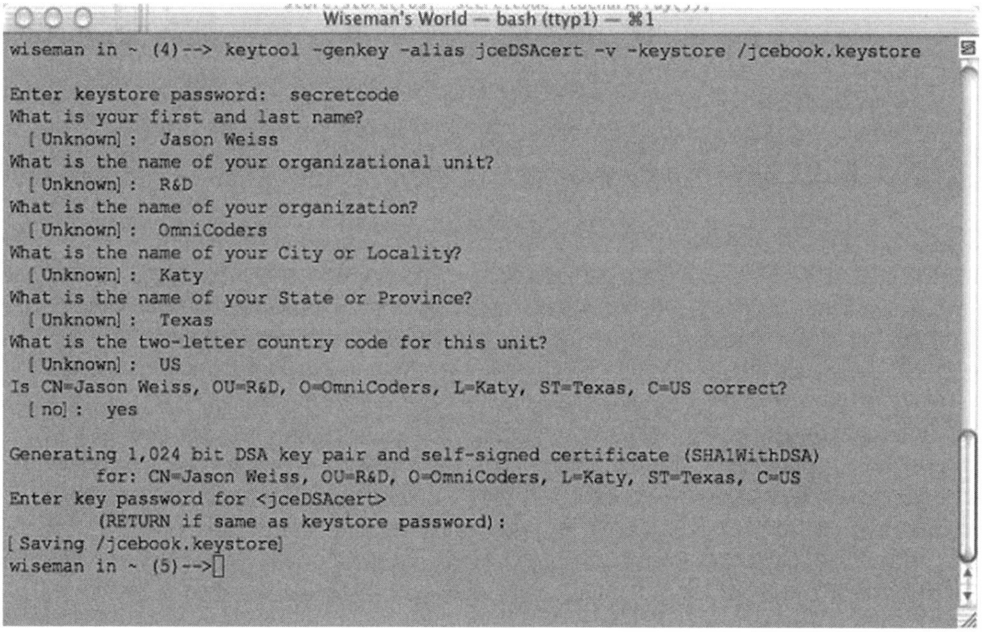

Figure 5.2: Creating a DSA certificate with a keytool.

would require the certificate be shipped off to a CA to be signed. However, for debugging and experimenting these untrusted certificates are more than adequate.

To create a digital certificate, just open up a shell window and execute the -genkey command as shown in Figure 5.2. By default, the genkey command will create a DSA certificate useful only for digital signatures, not encryption. The keytool uses the **alias** to represent the common name we will use to retrieve the certificate from the key store, either via keytool on the command line or programmatically.

We need to create an additional certificate that uses an RSA algorithm. Recall that RSA keys support digital signatures and encryption. The command you want to issue is nearly identical to the one we just completed in Figure 5-1. There are two differences, we are going to change the alias name and add a new flag to the command line to request a particular algorithm. The command looks like this:

```
keytool -genkey -alias jceRSAcert -v -keyalg RSA -keystore /jcebook.keystore
```

At this point, we should have two certificates in our key store, both using 1024-bit keys as echoed out on the verbose feedback presented by adding the -v flag to the command. KeyStore implementations actually supports storage of two types of objects, certificates/keys and trusted certificates preferably signed by a CA. For simplicity, this chapter will refer to keys and assume you understand that includes trusted certificates as well. The term *trusted certificate* is actually very misleading to the Java key store un-indoctrinated. There is no algorithm inside of the KeyStore implementation that verifies the certificate's public key is indeed associated with the *subject* named on the digital certificate; this is one of those people boundaries PC's simply can't tackle today. The question is do you believe the certificate is authentic? Perhaps this means at your organization simply checking to see if a CA has signed the certificate. Regardless of the litmus test applied, if you load it into the store as a trusted certificate, the key store is going to blindly trust you that everything is kosher and authentic. The moral of the story: never blindly trust that a certificate is authentic, because the KeyStore isn't going to speak up and tell you otherwise!

Let's list out the contents of our key store. To do this, we use the methods from our first code example, in addition to the new aliases() method that enumerates all of the entries.

Example 5.2 Sample Code Location: com.mkp.jce.chap5.ListKeyStoreContents

```
1  try
2  {
3  String defaultKeyStoreFormat = Security.getProperty("keystore.type");
4  KeyStore store = KeyStore.getInstance(defaultKeyStoreFormat);
5  FileInputStream fis = new FileInputStream(new File("/jcebook.keystore"));
6
7  char[] password = new char[] {'s','e','c','r','e','t','c','o','d','e'};
8  store.load(fis, password);
9  Arrays.fill(password, '\u0000');
10
11  for(Enumeration e = store.aliases();e.hasMoreElements();)
12  {
13     String name = (String) e.nextElement();
14     System.out.print("Located alias " + name);
15     System.out.println(" of type " +
16             ((store.isKeyEntry(name))
17                   ? " key/certificate"
18                   : " trusted certificate"));
19  }
20 } catch (KeyStoreException kse)
```

```
21 {
22  kse.printStackTrace();
23 } catch (FileNotFoundException fnfe)
24 {
25  fnfe.printStackTrace();
26 } catch (NoSuchAlgorithmException nse)
27 {
28  nse.printStackTrace();
29 } catch (CertificateException ce)
30 {
31  ce.printStackTrace();
32 } catch (IOException ioe)
33 {
34  ioe.printStackTrace();
35 }
```

Lines 3 through 6 are identical to what we covered before, opening up the key store. Be sure to experiment by typing in the wrong password. The KeyStore engine should throw an exception similar to this:

```
java.io.IOException: Keystore was tampered with, or password was incorrect
```

In line 11 we enumerate the known aliases in the key store, and we print out the alias names and their type-certificate/key or trusted certificate. On line 16, we determine their type by using one of the KeyStore helper methods, isKeyEntry(). At this point, we only have certificate/keys.

5.3.2   Code Example: Storage of a Symmetric Cipher Key

Despite Sun documentation and the intent of the KeyStore engine, the JKS key store format doesn't appear to support the storage of symmetric keys. There are references on the web from *years* ago, and while writing this book I could store the symmetric key into a JKS key store but could never retrieve it from the key store. It cites some exception regarding too much data being fed into the DER certificate (paraphrasing) (symmetric keys don't rely on or use a DER encoded certificate). If you need to store your symmetric keys in a key store, use the JCEKS or a third party provider.

In the following code examples, we register the Bouncy Castle provider, creating a new "BKS" formatted key store that will hold our symmetric key. Let's look at the code:

Example 5.3 Sample Code Location: com.mkp.jce.chap5.SecretKeyStorage

```
1   try
2   {
3       File file = new File("/jcebook.BKSkeystore");
4
5       //Dynamically register our Bouncy Castle provider
6       //without requiring java.security modification
7       //Place the provider in the fifth position
8       Provider bcProv =
9           new org.bouncycastle.jce.provider.BouncyCastleProvider();
10      Security.insertProviderAt(bcProv, 5);
11
12      //For demo purposes- in prod use real [] and null out after
13      //prompting user for the password
14      char[] secretcode = new char[] {'s','e','c','r','e','t','c','o','d','e'};
15
16      //The JKS format has problems (despite its stated abilities)
17      //handling symmetric keys. Using the BKS which works properly
18      KeyStore store = KeyStore.getInstance("BKS");
19
20      //Create the new BKS keystore
21      store.load(null, new char[0]);
22
23      KeyGenerator kg = KeyGenerator.getInstance("DES");
24      SecretKey key = kg.generateKey();
25      byte[] desKey = key.getEncoded();
26
27      //Convert the bytes to a SecretKeySpec
```

```
28      //continue with encryption operation from here
29
30      //now, save the DES key for future use in the keystore
31      //we will use the same password as the keystore, though
32      //not required and may often be a different password
33      store.setKeyEntry("myDESKey", key, secretcode, null);
34
35      //Remember, key store manipulation is done in-memory and only
36      //persisted to disk when the store() method is invoked!
37      FileOutputStream fos = new FileOutputStream(file);
38      store.store(fos, secretcode);
39      Arrays.fill(secretcode, '\u0000');
40      System.out.println("Key 'myDESKey' stored and written to disk.");
41
42 } catch (KeyStoreException kse)
43 {
44      kse.printStackTrace();
45 } catch (FileNotFoundException fnfe)
46 {
47      fnfe.printStackTrace();
48 } catch (NoSuchAlgorithmException nse)
49 {
50      nse.printStackTrace();
51 } catch (CertificateException ce)
52 {
53      ce.printStackTrace();
54 } catch (IOException ioe)
55  {
56      ioe.printStackTrace();
57 }
```

On line 18, we request a BKS formatted key store instance. Since this is a Bouncy Castle specific format, we know that the BC provider will respond. Line 21 creates a new key store by passing a null FileInputStream. Lines 23 through 25 are code identical to that which we worked with in Chapter 2, effectively creating a random DES symmetric key for use in a Cipher engine. We can imagine that lines 27 and 28 expand out into the full encryption routine, saving the ciphertext. At the conclusion of the encryption routine, we want to store our DES key for future use in decrypting that ciphertext. On line 33, we assign the alias *myDESKey* to our raw key bytes and protect it behind the "secretcode" password. Its imperative to remember that key operations always occur in memory, and unless an explicit store() method invocation is made, the key would be lost at the end of the program. We store out the key in our BKS formatted key store on line 38.

5.3.3 Code Example: Retrieving a Symmetric Cipher Key

The ability to retrieve the DES key from our previous example at a later point in time is crucial if we ever hope to decrypt the ciphertext from the imaginary encryption operation. Accessing the key is fairly trivial:

Example 5.4 Sample Code Location: com.mkp.jce.chap5.SecretKeyRetrieval

```
1   try
2   {
3       File file = new File("/jcebook.BKSkeystore");
4
5       Provider bcProv =
6               new org.bouncycastle.jce.provider.BouncyCastleProvider();
7       Security.insertProviderAt(bcProv, 5);
8
9       //For demo purposes- in prod use real [] and null out after
10      //prompting user for the value
11      char[] secretcode = new char[] {'s','e','c','r','e','t','c','o','d','e'};
12      KeyStore store = KeyStore.getInstance("BKS");
13      FileInputStream fis = new FileInputStream(file);
14      store.load(fis, secretcode);
15
16      Key key = store.getKey("myDESKey", secretcode);
```

```
17      byte[] desKey = key.getEncoded();
18      System.out.println("Key Loaded:");
19      for(int i=0;i<desKey.length;i++)
20      {
21              System.out.print(desKey[i] + " ");
22      }
23      System.out.println("");
24
25      Arrays.fill(secretcode, '\u0000');
26      //Convert the bytes to a SecretKeySpec and continue with decrypt
27
28 } catch (KeyStoreException kse)
29 {
30      kse.printStackTrace();
31 } catch (FileNotFoundException fnfe)
32 {
33      fnfe.printStackTrace();
34 } catch (NoSuchAlgorithmException nse)
35 {
36      nse.printStackTrace();
37 } catch (CertificateException ce)
38 {
39      ce.printStackTrace();
40 } catch (IOException ioe)
41 {
42      ioe.printStackTrace();
43 } catch (UnrecoverableKeyException uke)
44 {
45      uke.printStackTrace();
46 }
```

We register the Bouncy Castle provider and open up the BKS formatted key store on lines 5 through 14. Next, we invoke the getKey() method on line 16, specifying which symmetric key we want by using the alias we assigned, in this case *myDESKey* and providing the password that was used to protect the key. I now have a Key representation of my raw bytes and can proceed with my decryption operation.

5.3.4   A Word on Key Store Password Management

If you've ever done anything on this little thing they call the web, then you are like me and have to remember passwords for everything from your favorite Java site to your bank's web site. To date, no one has truly created a ubiquitous password management solution that everyone uses. The reality is that the key store itself is password protected, and I personally fail to see why individual keys need to also be password protected. Some have taken the position that there could be an IT department key store and certain keys are used by certain administrators, and hence the extra level of password protection. That argument doesn't convince me of the need. If different people need access to different keys, then just create another key store. The amount of time spent on password management is too high already, and for that reason, you may consider using the same password used to protect the key store to protect all of the items stored in the key store.

5.4   **The** CertificateFactory **Engine**

Most often you'll receive a certificate and not create it manually using the keytool utility. How you receive it is beyond our scope, but perhaps it will be received via e-mail, someone places it out on a shared drive, etc. There are two common formats for making a digital certificate mobile and ready for transport. The first is to extract out the bytes and use **distinguished encoding rules** (DER); the other is to Base64 encode a DER encoded certificate. Either approach can be read successfully via the CertificateFactory engine. To run some code examples that demonstrate reading certificates of both types, we need some more certificates! We return to our trusty keytool utility to help out here, and we can export out our existing certificates to the file system.

In Figure 5.3, we export the jceRSAcert alias using a DER format, and the jceDSAcert alias using a Base64 encoding. Both files are written out of the root in this example. With these certificates exported, we can now look at code examples for reading in each of these formats.

Example 5.5 Sample Code Location: com.mkp.jce.chap5.ReadDERCertificate

```
1  try
2  {
3      CertificateFactory factory = CertificateFactory.getInstance("X.509");
4
```

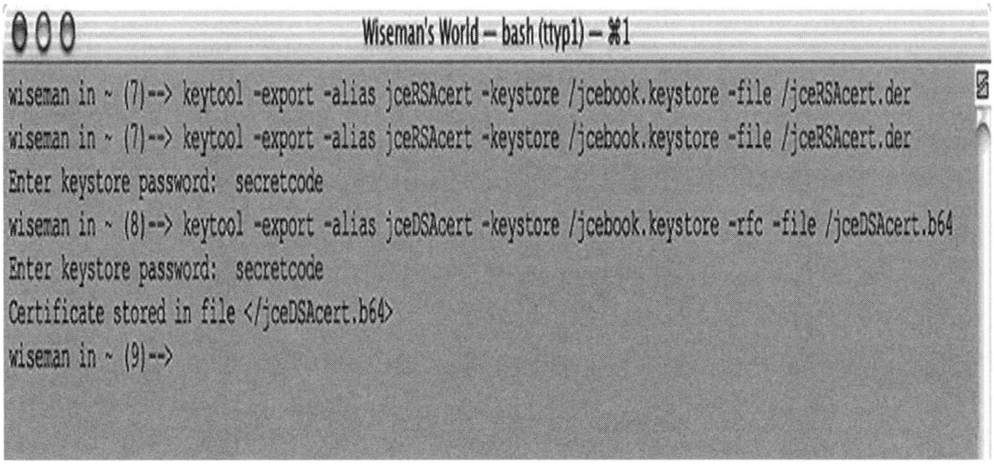

```
○ ○ ○                    Wiseman's World — bash (ttyp1) — ⌘1

wiseman in ~ (7)--> keytool -export -alias jceRSAcert -keystore /jcebook.keystore -file /jceRSAcert.der
wiseman in ~ (7)--> keytool -export -alias jceRSAcert -keystore /jcebook.keystore -file /jceRSAcert.der
Enter keystore password:  secretcode
wiseman in ~ (8)--> keytool -export -alias jceDSAcert -keystore /jcebook.keystore -rfc -file /jceDSAcert.b64
Enter keystore password:  secretcode
Certificate stored in file </jceDSAcert.b64>
wiseman in ~ (9)-->
```

Figure 5.3: Exporting digital certificates.

```
5       FileInputStream fis = new FileInputStream(new File("/jcebook.der"));

6

7       Certificate cert = factory.generateCertificate(fis);

8

9       System.out.println("Certificate Loaded:\n" + cert.toString());

10      fis.close();

11

12 } catch (CertificateException ce)

13 {

14      ce.printStackTrace();

15 } catch (FileNotFoundException fnfe)

16 {

17      fnfe.printStackTrace();

18 } catch (IOException ioe)

19 {

20      ioe.printStackTrace();

21 }
```

When a certificate is exported using DER syntax, reading it into a Java program and working with it is a trivial operation, especially compared with the steps required to process a Base64 encoded certificate. The DSA and the RSA certificates are represented as X.509 certificates. We request a CertificateFactory instance on line 3 that is capable of processing X.509 certificates. Once we have this instance, we invoke generateCertificate() on line 7, passing in the FileInputStream from line 5. At this point, we now have a generic Certificate object that contains all of the certificate's data.

Example 5.6 Sample Code Location: com.mkp.jce.chap5.ReadBase64Encoded

```
1   try
2   {
3        CertificateFactory factory =
4                CertificateFactory.getInstance("X.509");
5
6        try
7        {
8            FileInputStream fis =
9                new FileInputStream(new File("/jceDSAcert.b64"));
10
11            try
12            {
13                DataInputStream dis = new DataInputStream(fis);
14
15                byte[] bytes = new byte[dis.available()];
16
17                try
18                {
19                    dis.readFully(bytes);
20                    ByteArrayInputStream bais =
21                        new ByteArrayInputStream(bytes);
22
23                    while (bais.available() > 0)
```

```
24                          {
25                                      Certificate cert =
26                                          factory.generateCertificate(bais);
27                                  System.out.println(cert.toString());
28                          }
29
30                  } catch (IOException ioe)
31                  {
32                          ioe.printStackTrace();
33                  } finally
34                  {
35                      try
36                      {
37                              dis.close();
38                              fis.close();
39                      } catch (Exception e)
40                      {
41                              //this is bad!
42                              e.printStackTrace();
43                      }
44                  }
45          } catch (IOException ioe)
46          {
47                  ioe.printStackTrace();
48          }
49
50  } catch (FileNotFoundException fnfe)
51  {
52          fnfe.printStackTrace();
53  }
```

```
54 } catch (CertificateException ce)

55 {

56     ce.printStackTrace();

57 }
```

The code to read a Base64 encoded certificate is over twice as long as the code required to read a DER encoded certificate. Base64 encoding is incredibly useful, as it's all printable characters. Many CAs will make a signed certificate available via a web site (after all the security checks are complete). They Base64 encode the certificate and display it inside of a large text box on the web page for you to copy and paste into a Notepad or your editor of choice and save out to your local disk drive. For this reason alone, having a utility to read a Base64 encoded certificate in your toolbox is essential. Most of the complexity in this sample is a result of exception handling. Essentially, on lines 3 and 4 we obtain our CertificateFactory instance. We open up a FileInputStream on lines 8 and 9, and read the raw bytes via a DataInputStream / ByteArrayInputStream set of pipes in lines 13 through 21. With the bytes available, we pass the ByteArrayInputStream into the factory's generateCertificate() method on lines 25 and 26. In our example, we know the Base64 encoded data only contains a single certificate, but we loop to demonstrate how to handle the situation if there were multiple certificates present.

5.4.1   Process for Requesting a Certificate Signed by a CA

The first step in obtaining a CA signed digital certificate is to find out what algorithms your CA supports; most will support RSA. Using the keytool utility, use the -genkey option to generate a private/public key pair, filling in each of the distinguished name fields if not provided on the command line. The command should look similar to this:

```
keytool -genkey -keyalg RSA -keysize 1024 -alias myCertKeyPair
```

Once you have your key pair generated, you again use the keytool, this time invoking the certificate request option, -certreq. The command should look like this:

```
keytool -certreq -alias myCertKeyPair -file /certreq.csr
```

The .csr extension stands for Certificate Signature Request. At this point, before getting more coffee, going to the bathroom, or taking that next breath—BACK UP YOUR KEY STORE! Remember, digital certificates contain the public key and meta-data about you. At no time do you distribute your private key, not even to a CA! Thus, if you lose the key pair that was generated, you lose the private key. The CA signed digital certificate becomes worthless without the private key that matches the public key embedded inside of the certificate. Without the private key you can't generate any digital signatures or perform encryption operations if the algorithm supports them. Now that your key store has been backed up, we can continue. After shipping off your .csr to your CA of choice, days (or weeks!) might pass before the CA believes you are who you say you are and signs your public key and the meta-data you provided. Once they do, you should receive a PKCS#7 formatted certificate complete with a certificate chain of who signed it. Depending on how the CA operates, they will provide you with a trusted certificate that will probably be either DER encoded or Base64 encoded. However, typically *you* won't be reading your own trusted certificate, you'll be reading your associate's trusted certificate or a business partner's certificate. Regardless of in which format they forward their trusted certificate over to you, we've already seen examples of how they can be read.

Remember, digital signatures use the private key (remember my big fit about backing up your key store!) not the public certificate. There really is little reason for *you* to be reading and working with the trusted certificate. Most likely, you'll be distributing your CA signed trusted certificate out to the people you'll be sending documents to.

5.4.2 Certificate Revocation List (CRL)

Once you receive a trusted certificate back from your CA, you distribute that public certificate out to perhaps thousands of business partners. Likewise, they distribute their certificates to their business partners, etc. Occasionally, a CA may realize it was a victim of fraud and determines it must *immediately* revoke a certificate that it issued where the listed expiration date could be two years in the future. The CA can't just physically pull the certificate; it doesn't know everyone who hass received that certificate. Instead, *each* CA must maintain what is known as a **Certificate Revocation List** (CRL), which, as the name implies, represents a list of revoked certificates that shouldn't be considered valid. None of the core Java security classes automatically download CRLs from CAs (though I have seen references to the storage of a CRL in a remote keystore using PKCS#7 format). It's impossible to expect such behavior, as there are so many CAs out there! Sadly, the implementation of a CRL is still very liquid and frankly, unreliable at times. The unreliability stems from the sheer number of places an application might have to look to ensure a certificate hasn't been revoked, for example 500 business partners could each theoretically give you a public certificate they expect you to trust, where more than 300 different CAs were used in the issuance of those trusted certificates. If only one of them is "slow" in keeping their public CRL list up-to-date, then the process suffers with little recourse.

Java represents revoked certificates using the X509CRLEntry class. Point your browser at https://www.thawte.com/cgi/lifecycle/roots.exe and scroll to the bottom—we need to download a .crl file from a CA to demonstrate CRL checking in Java. Grab their *Thawte Server CA* .crl file and save it to your root directory (or modify the following code sample).

Example 5.7 Sample Code Location: com.mkp.jce.chap5.ProcessCRLFromCA

```
1   try
2   {
```

```
3      FileInputStream fis =
4              new FileInputStream(new File("/ThawteServerCA.crl"));
5      CertificateFactory factory = CertificateFactory.getInstance("X.509");
6      X509CRL crl = (X509CRL) factory.generateCRL(fis);
7      fis.close();
8
9      Set crlSet = crl.getRevokedCertificates();
10     Iterator iter = crlSet.iterator();
11     while(iter.hasNext())
12     {
13             X509CRLEntry entry = (X509CRLEntry) iter.next();
14             System.out.print("Certificate with serial #");
15             System.out.print(entry.getSerialNumber());
16             System.out.print(" was revoked on ");
17             System.out.println(entry.getRevocationDate());
18     }
19
20 } catch (FileNotFoundException fnfe)
21 {
22     fnfe.printStackTrace();
23 } catch (CertificateException ce)
24 {
25     ce.printStackTrace();
26 } catch (CRLException crle)
27 {
28     crle.printStackTrace();
29 } catch (IOException ioe)
30 {
31     ioe.printStackTrace();
32 }
```

This small code example passes a FileInputStream that maps to the CA's CRL into the CertificateFactory instance via the factory's generateCRL() method. Invoking this method processes the CRL and collects all of the data into a single X509CRL instance. In this case, we iterate over the CRL itself to show all of the revoked certificates. A revoked certificate typically only stays in this list until the certificate expires, at which point it is assumed that anyone looking to use the certificate will disallow its usage because it has expired. Sample output is row after row of data like this:

```
Certificate with serial #641412 was revoked on Mon Dec 23 03:46:47 CST 2002

Certificate with serial #621402 was revoked on Wed Feb 19 22:39:32 CST 2003

Certificate with serial #608623 was revoked on Thu Feb 27 17:08:27 CST 2003
```

While we showed the serial number of the certificate, in most cases what occurs is that a certificate is loaded, and that in-memory Certificate instance is validated against the CRL by inspecting the result of the isRevoked() method:

```
boolean isRevoked = crl.isRevoked(certificate);
```

Many of the major CAs have already moved past manual downloads of CRL data into something known as **Online Certificate Status Protocol** (OCSP). OCSP overcomes the whole download requirement because it is a real-time, on-line protocol. OCSP is simple; when a client attempts to access a resource identified by a certificate, a request is sent for certificate status information. The CA server responds back with one of "current," "expired," or "unknown." Google searches restricted to *http://java.sun.com* reveal a number of OCSP hits, most of which are from old JavaOne sessions or BOFs with a slide title like "Possible Future Directions." At this point, there isn't any conclusive information on when the JCA will formally support the OCSP protocol. Bouncy Castle added support for OCSP with the introduction of version 1.19.

5.4.3   Code Example: Encryption with a Digital Certificate

Let's revise one of our Cipher engine examples, this time using a digital certificate to prime the engine for an encryption operation. Recall that each digital certificate includes a public key. The Cipher engine overloads the init() method to accept a Certificate instance. Let's encrypt some data:

Example 5.8 Sample Code Location: com.mkp.jce.chap5.CertificateEncryptionDemo

```
1   //Dynamically register our Bouncy Castle

2   //provider without requiring java.security modification

3   //Place the provider in the fifth position

4   Provider bcProv = new org.bouncycastle.jce.provider.BouncyCastleProvider();
```

```
5  Security.insertProviderAt(bcProv, 5);

6  System.out.println("Registered BC provider successfully");

7

8  //Dynamically register our Cryptix

9  //provider without requiring java.security modification

10 //Place the provider in the sixth position

11 Provider cryptixProv = new cryptix.jce.provider.CryptixCrypto();

12 Security.insertProviderAt(cryptixProv, 6);

13 System.out.println("Registered Cryptix provider successfully");

14

15

16 try

17 {

18     CertificateFactory factory = CertificateFactory.getInstance("X.509");

19

20     FileInputStream fis = new FileInputStream(new File("/jceRSAcert.der"));

21

22     Certificate cert = factory.generateCertificate(fis);

23

24     System.out.println("Certificate Loaded.");

25     fis.close();

26

27     //Locate an RSA cipher engine

28     //initialize it using the public key for encryption

29     Cipher cipher = Cipher.getInstance("RSA/ECB/PKCS#1");

30     cipher.init(Cipher.ENCRYPT_MODE, cert);

31

32     String plainText = "This is my secret message";

33

34     //Generate the cipher text
```

```
35      byte[] cipherText = cipher.doFinal(plainText.getBytes("UTF-8"));

36

37      //In the interest of brevity, use CryptoUtil to write the ciphertext file

38      CryptoUtil.writeCipherTextFile(

39              new File("/ciphertext.cert.dat"), cipherText);

40

41      System.out.println("See \ciphertext.cert.dat for the encrypted text.");

42

43 } catch (IOException ioe)

44 {

45      ioe.printStackTrace();

46 } catch (NoSuchAlgorithmException nsae)

47 {

48      nsae.printStackTrace();

49 } catch (NoSuchPaddingException nspe)

50 {

51      nspe.printStackTrace();

52 } catch (InvalidKeyException ike)

53 {

54      ike.printStackTrace();

55 } catch (IllegalStateException ise)

56 {

57      ise.printStackTrace();

58 } catch (CertificateException ce)

59 {

60      ce.printStackTrace();

61 } catch (IllegalBlockSizeException ibse)

62 {

63      ibse.printStackTrace();

64 } catch (BadPaddingException bpe)
```

```
65 {

66     bpe.printStackTrace();

67 }
```

Line 18 requests an X.509 CertificateFactory instance that is used on line 22 to extract our certificate from the FileInputStream. Once we have the certificate, the only variance in encryption is found on line 30 where we pass the certificate in place of the key into the init() method of the Cipher engine.

5.4.4   Code Example: Decryption with a Private Key

To reiterate an important point, a digital certificate includes the public key and a series of name-value pairs, and a trusted certificate is digitally signed by a CA. Nowhere in the digital certificate is the private key present. However, when you generated the certificate originally a private key had to be generated alongside the public key. This private key remains stowed away inside of your key store. Using the alias we entered when we executed the keytool –genkey option, we can access the private key to perform a decryption operation. It also goes without saying that if you lose the key store and the private key, then the certificate (trusted or not) immediately becomes worthless! The morale of the story is to protect your key store, especially if it contains the private key of a publicly distributed trusted certificate.

Example 5.9 Sample Code Location: com.mkp.jce.chap5.PrivateKeyDecryptionDemo

```
1   Provider bcProv = new org.bouncycastle.jce.provider.BouncyCastleProvider();

2   Security.insertProviderAt(bcProv, 5);

3   System.out.println("Registered BC provider successfully");

4

5   Provider cryptixProv = new cryptix.jce.provider.CryptixCrypto();

6   Security.insertProviderAt(cryptixProv, 6);

7   System.out.println("Registered Cryptix provider successfully");

8

9   try

10  {

11      KeyStore store = KeyStore.getInstance(KeyStore.getDefaultType());

12      FileInputStream fis = new FileInputStream(new File("/jcebook.keystore"));
```

```
13
14     char[] secretcode = new char[] {'s','e','c','r','e','t','c','o','d','e'};
15     store.load(fis, secretcode);
16
17     //we used the keystore password to protect the key as well
18     RSAPrivateKey privKey = (RSAPrivateKey)
19             store.getKey("jceRSAcert", secretcode);
20     Arrays.fill(secretcode, '\u0000');
21     System.out.println("Loaded RSA Private Key!!");
22
23     //Locate an RSA cipher engine
24     //initialize it using the public key for encryption
25     Cipher cipher = Cipher.getInstance("RSA/ECB/PKCS#1");
26     cipher.init(Cipher.DECRYPT_MODE, privKey);
27
28     byte[] cipherText =
29             CryptoUtil.readCipherTextFile(new File("/ciphertext.cert.dat"));
30
31     //Generate the cipher text
32     byte[] plainTextBytes = cipher.doFinal(cipherText);
33
34     String plainText = new String(plainTextBytes);
35     System.out.println("Decrypted Plain Text:\n" + plainText);
36
37 } catch (KeyStoreException kse)
38 {
39     kse.printStackTrace();
40 } catch (FileNotFoundException fnfe)
41 {
42     fnfe.printStackTrace();
```

```
43 } catch (NoSuchAlgorithmException nsae)
44 {
45     nsae.printStackTrace();
46 } catch (CertificateException ce)
47 {
48     ce.printStackTrace();
49 } catch (IOException ioe)
50 {
51     ioe.printStackTrace();
52 } catch (UnrecoverableKeyException uke)
53 {
54     uke.printStackTrace();
55 } catch (NoSuchPaddingException nspe)
56 {
57     nspe.printStackTrace();
58 } catch (InvalidKeyException ike)
59 {
60     ike.printStackTrace();
61 } catch (IllegalStateException ise)
62 {
63     ise.printStackTrace();
64 } catch (IllegalBlockSizeException ibse)
65 {
66     ibse.printStackTrace();
67 } catch (BadPaddingException bpe)
68 {
69     bpe.printStackTrace();
70 }
```

We load our key store on lines 11 through 15. We extract our RSAPrivateKey by invoking the getKey() method on our key store instance on lines 18 and 19. We use the same alias name we entered on the keytool utility. If you flip back to Figure 5-1 where we created a DSA key pair, notice the very last line that reads *Enter key password for <alias name>*. While it is possible to assign individual passwords to protect keys above and beyond the keystore password, we chose to reuse the key store password.

You may be wondering why the password is a char[] instead of a String. Recall that String objects in Java are immutable. Thus, there is no way to "zero-out" a String object after it has been used. Production systems need to reset the char[] values to null to ensure someone sniffing the PC's memory couldn't locate the password after the program had run.

Once we have the RSAPrivateKey in hand, the decryption operation begins on line 25 and is identical to previous examples.

5.4.5   RSA Encryption Limitations

Every RSA initialization process requires the random selection of two very large primes, traditionally referred to as *p* and *q*, and computing *n* such that *n=pq*. Previously, we extolled the virtues of RSA over DSA, citing that RSA could be used for encryption and digital signature applications, while DSA was strictly for digital signature applications. In the real world, the encryption capabilities of RSA are rarely used for one simple reason: the length of the plaintext that can be encrypted is limited to the size of *n*. In fact, the real length is even smaller than *n* because of the overhead introduced by the algorithms. As a result, the predominate approach is to generate a random secret key and encrypt that key with the RSA keys. The message is then encrypted using a symmetric cipher with the generated secret key. The net-net is that two pieces of information are then sent over the wire. Let's talk about an example using Alice and Bob.

5.4.6   Code Example: Combining RSA with a Secret Key

Alice wants to send Bob a confidential report. She already has a copy of Bob's digital certificate, stored as a trusted certificate in her key store. Alice uses a KeyGenerator to randomly generate a secret key that can be fed into a symmetric cipher. Using the public key from Bob's digital certificate, she encrypts the secret key and stores the result in a file called secretkey.dat. She then uses an AES cipher to encrypt the report using the secret key and stores the ciphertext in a file called encrypted_report.dat. In an e-mail, she attaches the secretkey.dat and the encrypted_report.dat files and addresses it to Bob. When Bob receives the e-mail, he uses his private key to decrypt the secretkey.dat file. Now Bob knows the secret key, and he can use that to decrypt and read the report. Even if the e-mail between Alice and Bob was intercepted by Eve, Eve doesn't have a copy of Bob's private key, and so it would be extremely difficult for Eve to decipher either encrypted file. Let's see two back-to-back code examples demonstrating a revised method of using RSA to protect the secret key.

Example 5.10 Sample Code Location: com.mkp.jce.chap5.SecretKeyOverRSAEncrypt

```
1  Provider bcProv = new org.bouncycastle.jce.provider.BouncyCastleProvider();
2  Security.insertProviderAt(bcProv, 5);
3  System.out.println("Registered BC provider successfully");
4
5  Provider cryptixProv = new cryptix.jce.provider.CryptixCrypto();
6  Security.insertProviderAt(cryptixProv, 6);
7  System.out.println("Registered Cryptix provider successfully");
8
9  try
10 {
11    Certificate cert =
12    CryptoUtil.readDerEncodedX509Certificate(new File("/jceRSAcert.der"));
13    System.out.println("Certificate Loaded.");
14
15    KeyGenerator kg = KeyGenerator.getInstance("AES");
16    SecretKey key = kg.generateKey();
17    byte[] aesKey = key.getEncoded();
18    SecretKeySpec keySpec = new SecretKeySpec(aesKey, "AES");
19
20    Cipher keyCipher = Cipher.getInstance("RSA/ECB/PKCS#1");
21    keyCipher.init(Cipher.ENCRYPT_MODE, cert);
22
23    byte[] keyCipherText = keyCipher.doFinal(aesKey);
24    CryptoUtil.writeCipherTextFile(
25            new File("/secretkey.dat"), keyCipherText);
26    System.out.println("Secret protected behind pubkey in /secretkey.dat");
27
28    Cipher msgCipher = Cipher.getInstance("AES");
29    msgCipher.init(Cipher.ENCRYPT_MODE, keySpec);
```

```
30
31     String plainText =
32             CryptoUtil.readPlainTextFile(new File("/velocity.log"));
33
34     byte[] msgCipherText = msgCipher.doFinal(plainText.getBytes());
35
36     CryptoUtil.writeCipherTextFile(new File("/message.dat"), msgCipherText);
37     System.out.println("Message encrypted and written to /message.dat");
38 } catch (IOException ioe)
39 {
40     ioe.printStackTrace();
41 } catch (NoSuchAlgorithmException nsae)
42 {
43     nsae.printStackTrace();
44 } catch (NoSuchPaddingException nspe)
45 {
46     nspe.printStackTrace();
47 } catch (InvalidKeyException ike)
48 {
49     ike.printStackTrace();
50 } catch (IllegalStateException ise)
51 {
52     ise.printStackTrace();
53 } catch (IllegalBlockSizeException ibse)
54 {
55     ibse.printStackTrace();
56 } catch (BadPaddingException bpe)
57 {
58     bpe.printStackTrace();
59 }
```

Example 5.11 Sample Code Location: com.mkp.jce.chap5.SecretKeyOverRSADecrypt

```
1   Provider bcProv = new org.bouncycastle.jce.provider.BouncyCastleProvider();
2   Security.insertProviderAt(bcProv, 5);
3   System.out.println("Registered BC provider successfully");
4
5   Provider cryptixProv = new cryptix.jce.provider.CryptixCrypto();
6   Security.insertProviderAt(cryptixProv, 6);
7   System.out.println("Registered Cryptix provider successfully");
8
9   try
10  {
11      KeyStore store = KeyStore.getInstance(KeyStore.getDefaultType());
12      FileInputStream fis = new FileInputStream(new File("/jcebook.keystore"));
13
14      char[] secretcode = new char[] {'s','e','c','r','e','t','c','o','d','e'};
15      store.load(fis, secretcode);
16      RSAPrivateKey privKey = (RSAPrivateKey)
17              store.getKey("jceRSAcert", secretcode);
18      Arrays.fill(secretcode, '\u0000');
19      System.out.println("Loaded RSA Private Key!!");
20
21      byte[] secretKey =
22              CryptoUtil.readCipherTextFile(new File("/secretkey.dat"));
23
24      Cipher keyCipher = Cipher.getInstance("RSA/ECB/PKCS#1");
25      keyCipher.init(Cipher.DECRYPT_MODE, privKey);
26      byte[] aesKey = keyCipher.doFinal(secretKey);
27
28      SecretKeySpec keySpec = new SecretKeySpec(aesKey, "AES");
29      System.out.println("Extracted the secret AES key using my private key");
```

```
30
31    byte[] cipherText =
32            CryptoUtil.readCipherTextFile(new File("/message.dat"));
33
34    Cipher msgCipher = Cipher.getInstance("AES");
35    msgCipher.init(Cipher.DECRYPT_MODE, keySpec);
36
37    byte[] plainTextBytes = msgCipher.doFinal(cipherText);
38    String plainText = new String(plainTextBytes);
39    System.out.println("Decrypted Message:\n" + plainText);
40 } catch (IOException ioe)
41 {
42    ioe.printStackTrace();
43 } catch (NoSuchAlgorithmException nsae)
44 {
45    nsae.printStackTrace();
46 } catch (NoSuchPaddingException nspe)
47 {
48    nspe.printStackTrace();
49 } catch (InvalidKeyException ike)
50 {
51    ike.printStackTrace();
52 } catch (IllegalStateException ise)
53 {
54    ise.printStackTrace();
55 } catch (IllegalBlockSizeException ibse)
56 {
57    ibse.printStackTrace();
58 } catch (BadPaddingException bpe)
59 {
```

```
60     bpe.printStackTrace();
61 } catch (KeyStoreException kse)
62 {
63     kse.printStackTrace();
64 } catch (CertificateException ce)
65 {
66     ce.printStackTrace();
67 } catch (UnrecoverableKeyException uke)
68 {
69     uke.printStackTrace();
70 }
```

At this point, there aren't any new engines to discuss or classes to introduce that we haven't seen before. In fact, these code examples represent the climax of our journey. These samples should encourage you to look at different ways you can combine the various building techniques covered throughout this book to achieve not just something that works but an *optimal solution* to the problem at hand. What is demonstrated here is a common and powerful technique for two parties who have previously exchanged public keys to securely communicate and share documents with one another. What technique could be used if Alice and Bob were strangers who wanted to securely share files on demand without requiring a previous exchange of digital certificates? (Take a minute to think about it...we'll discuss the answer shortly.)

The elegance in these samples lies in the fact that they leverage the strengths of multiple engines, resolving a would-be RSA encryption size restriction problem. We enjoy the speed, security, and flexibility of the AES symmetric cipher, without having to invent creative ways of sharing the key—we just encrypt it using the receiver's public key!

Previously, I asked what technique we could use if Alice and Bob were strangers. The answer hopefully doesn't shock you; introduce a key exchange algorithm like the DH example found in Chapter 3.

5.5 Conclusion

What a journey! We covered over a dozen engines and all of their related interfaces, classes, and surrounding terminology. With a little help from Alice and Bob, we've demonstrated numerous ways of keeping Eve's nose where it doesn't belong. I want to take this opportunity to again emphasize the planning that went into the code samples so they could be copied and pasted into your classes to save you some time. If you haven't downloaded them yet for your toolbox, what are you waiting for!? Flip back to the Preface now for download directions.

Keep those keys secure and your key stores backed up!

Bibliography

[1] Java Cryptography Architecture API Specification & Reference,
   http://java.sun.com/j2se/1.4.2/docs/guide/security/CryptoSpec.html

[2] Using the BootClasspath,
   http://www.javageeks.com/Papers/BootClasspath/BootClasspath.pdf

[3] Java Extensions FAQ,
   http://java.sun.com/products/jdk/1.2/docs/guide/extensions/ext_faq.html

[4] Multipurpose Internet Mail Extensions(MIME) Part One: Format of Internet Message Bodies,
   http://www.ietf.org/rfc/rfc2045.txt

[5] Java Cryptography Extension Reference Guide,
   http://java.sun.com/j2se/1.4.2/docs/guide/security/jce/JCERefGuide.html

[6] Jerrold Grossman, Section 4.1 *The Idea of an Algorithm*, "Discrete Mathematics," 1990, page 219.

[7] Should one test for weak keys in DES?
   http://www.rsasecurity.com/rsalabs/faq/3-2-4.html

[8] FIPS 74-Guidelines for Implementing and Using the NBS Data,
   http://www.itl.nist.gov/fipspubs/fip74.htm

[9] Bruce Schneier, Section 14.3 *Blowfish*, "Applied Cryptography," 1996, page 336.

[10] Data encryption for J2ME Profiles, http://wireless.java.sun.com/midp/ttips/dataencryp

[11] Bruce Schneier, Section 3.2 *Authentication*, "Applied Cryptography," 1996, page 52.

[12] Bruce Schneier, Section 9.3 *Cipher Block Chaining Mode*, "Applied Cryptography," 1996, page 194.

[13] Password Based Encryption,
http://www.rsasecurity.com/solutions/developers/whitepapers/Article3-PBE.pdf

[14] One-way Hash Functions, http://home.ecn.ab.ca/~jsavard/crypto/mi0605.htm

[15] C Implementation of NSA's Secure Hash Algorithm,
http://www.cc.utah.edu/~nahaj/c/sha/

[16] Niels Ferguson and Bruce Schneier, Section 13.4 *RSA Defined*, "Practical Cryptography," 2003, page 229.

[17] What is the AES?, http://www.rsasecurity.com/rsalabs/faq/3-3-1.html

[18] A Comparison of RSA and Elliptic Curve Encryption,
http://www.cs.uct.ac.za/courses/CS400W/NIS/papers00/mlesaoan/paper.html

[19] Gamma, E., Helm, R., Johnson, R. & Vlissides, J. (1995). Design patterns: Elements of reusable object-oriented software. Reading, MA: Addison Wesley.

[20] What are MD2, MD4, and MD5?
http://www.rsasecurity.com/rsalabs/faq/3-6-6.html

[21] Bert den Boer and Antoon Bosselaers, Collisions for the compression function of MD5. In Tor Helleseth, editor, Advances in Cryptology-EUROCRYPT '93, volume 765 of Lecture Notes in Computer Science, pages 293–304. Springer-Verlag, 1993.

[22] David Wagner and Bruce Schneier. Analysis of the SSL 3.0 protocol. In *Proceedings of the Second USENIX Workshop on Electronic Commerce,* pages 29–40. USENIX Press, November 1996. Revised version available from http://www.counterpane.com

[23] Research and Development in Advanced Communication Technologies in Europe, *RIPE Integrity Primitives: Final Report of RACE Integrity Primitives Evaluation (R1040)*, RACE, June 1992.

[24] What are DSA and DSS?
http://www.rsasecurity.com/rsalabs/faq/3-4-1.html

[25] D. Kahn. (1967). The Codebreakers: The Story of Secret Writing. New York: Macmillan.

[26] B. Schneier. Section 2.3 *One-Way Functions*, "Applied Cryptography," 1996, page 29.

Index

155

The Morgan Kaufmann Practical Guides

Series Editor: Michael J. Donahoo

JSP: Practical Guide for Java Programmers
by Robert J. Brunner

With JSP, business systems can be leveraged with minimal overhead, maintenance, and support. This book covers the latest release of JSP, version 2.0, including new features such as the Expression Language, the JSP Standard Tag Library, and Tag Files.

JSTL: Practical Guide for JSP Programmers
by Sue Spielman

"An invaluable reference for any JSP developer's library. Sue makes the complicated seem simple with her conversational writing style and well thought out examples and analogies."

> —**Matt Houser,** J2EE Developer with The Washington Post and former Sun Microsystems Java Instructor

TCP/IP Sockets in Java: Practical Guide for Programmers
by Kenneth L. Calvert and Michael J. Donahoo

This easy-to-use book consists of a concise yet very thorough tutorial with examples and reference material that help readers learn and practice specific TCP/IP socket programming techniques. As a result, readers are able to grasp the practical applications of using the TCP/IP protocol and use this understanding as a springboard for more advanced assignments, including multimedia protocols.